CROMFORD

B

PETER J NAYLOR
GSC Ieng BA BSc G4txq MSOE/MIPlantE ACIBSE

New Edition
© Peter Naylor 2001
Reprinted with amendment 2005

The rights of the author of this work have been asserted by him in accordance with the Copyright, Design and Patents Act, 1993.

All rights reserved. No part of this publication may be reproduced, stored in a retrieval system or transmitted in any form or by any means, electronic, mechanical, photocopying, recording or otherwise without the prior permission of Watnay Publishing.

British Library Cataloguing in Publication data: catalogue record for this book is available from the British Library.

ISBN 1 872 418 05 8

Published by Watnay Publishing
An Imprint of Peter J Naylor Ltd
24 Castle View Drive
Cromford
Matlock
DE4 3RL

This book was typeset, printed and bound by: Drummond Print and Design Ltd. Bakewell Road, Matlock, DE4 3AU

Originally published by
Happy Walking International Ltd. 1999, ISBN 1 84173 007 6

Other Books by Watnay Publishing:

Spondon – a History
Derbyshire Graves
Mickleover and Littleover – a History
Beetroot and other stories
Let not your heart be troubled
Flesh and Blood
Chaddesden - a History

Other books by Peter J Naylor

Discover Dowsing and Divining
Discover Lost Mines
Ancient Wells and Springs of Derbyshire
Celtic Derbyshire
Manors and Families of Derbyshire (two volumes)
Grandfather Thomas Jackson's Recipes
Derbyshire Graves
The Derbyshire Connections of the Stokely family of Iowa, USA
Map of Ashbourne, 1900
The Lost Villages of Derbyshire
The Millennium Book of Belper (Editor and contributor)
Well Dressing (With Lindsey Porter)
History of the Matlocks Water Supply

Commissioning Specialists' Association – Technical Memoranda
    TM3: Design of Standard Test Sheets
    TM7 ; Steam and the Commissioning Engineer
    TM9: Water Treatment and the Commissioning Engineer

Articles in:

    The Bulletin of the Peak District Mines Society
    Derbyshire Countryside
    Derbyshire Miscellany
    The Ghost Club Magazine

Contents

Other books by Peter J Naylor		ii
Contents		4
Introduction		6
Chapter One It might have been a Manchester!		8
Chapter Two The Romans, the Normans and beyond		13
Chapter Three Mining		19
Chapter Four The Age of Arkwright		31
Chapter Five Arkwright's Legacy		49
Chapter Six Transport		56
Chapter Seven Buildings		69
Chapter Eight Cromford apart from the Arkwrights		86
Appendices		
I	Monuments and Memorials - St Mary's Church	93
II	A Pedigree of the Arkwright Family	98
III	A Pedigree of the Hurt Family	99
IV	List of prizes for Market Traders, Cromford Market – 1790	100
V	Incumbents of the Parish Church of St Mary, Cromford	101
VI	Cromford in Germany	103
VII	Original water sources for Cromford	104
VIII	War Memorials -Cromford	105
	Scarthin	106
Places to Visit		107
A walk around the Cromford Area		113
Bibliography		116
Acknowledgements		118

© Cambridge University Collection of Air Photographs

An aerial photograph of Cromford 9th April 1990. This clearly shows the River Derwent, Bonsall Hollow and the route of the Cromford and High Peak Railway. The roads in and out of the village are also evident. The square in the grass on the Meadow was where an RASC camp existed for the Second World War.

Introduction

This is the story of a village, the village the writer chose to live in, for no better reason than he wished to. His first meeting with Cromford was when, at the age of twelve in 1948, he stayed at Willersley Castle. His abiding memory of this stay was waking up one morning and on looking out of his room - which he shared with another boy who was to become his "best Man" in 1958 - the scene which greeted him was a world of white. It had snowed heavily and the hills and trees were covered in white as far as the eye could see. He was mesmerised and vowed there and then that one day, he would live here. After an interval of forty years he achieved his dream and he does not intend to leave.

This village is unique, but then all villages are. Cromford stands out because of what happened here towards the end of the eighteenth century and the efforts of one man, Sir Richard Arkwright. Many men have shaped the villages they have owned, but none more than this man. Substantially, the village the visitor sees today is this man's village and his influence was so profound that a history of the place must for the most part be the story of Arkwright.

Cromford is gifted by lying in a beautiful valley, surrounded by hills and cliffs, well watered with good communications. It is also a home for many people, most work but many are retired and many of these are newcomers, bewitched by the charms of the area. People come on day excursions to look at the mills or walk the many scenic paths that abound in the area, for this is a walkers' county. The visitor is spoiled for choice, for the charms of the place range from climbing the Black Rocks (originally named Stonnis), to fishing in the river, looking at the old cotton mills or climbing Sheep Pasture Incline to Cromford Moor.

Whatever the tastes of the visitor, he is provided for - good pubs which supply good ale, places to eat, places to dream and places to stay.

The author has written this book as an act of love, by way of saying thank you to the village and its people for having him in their midst. It was written from his home with a view which takes the eye to the hillside above the Meadows and up to Bilberry Knoll, along Matlock Gorge and over to Masson Hill. Was there ever a better view from a house?

This same view would have been familiar to the Arkwrights, Allison Uttley and any rambler who ventures up Intake Lane.

At the time of going to press, the Derwent valley from Masson Mill, Matlock Bath to the Silk Mill, Derby, is under consideration for World Heritage status. This puts the valley, including Cromford, on a par with Stonehenge and the Pyramids.

A note: Sir Richard Arkwright is referred to as such or just Arkwright. His only son is referred to as Richard Junior or Jnr or Richard II, and his grandson and son of Richard II as Richard III. Also references to Mill Lane also refer to Mill Road and vice versa.

PJN
Cromford
September, 2001

Footnote:

The following books are recommended which could be enjoyed together with this history:

Memories of Cromford	Cromford Womens' Institute	2000
Our Village – Allison Uttley's Cromford	Scarthin Books	1987
The Cromford Guide	Freda Bayles and Janet Ede Scarthin Books	1994
Transformation of a Valley	Brian and Neville Cooper Scarthin Books	1991

Chapter One
It might have been a Manchester!

To a traveller in the first half of the 18th Century, Cromford would have appeared as a collection of cottages, mostly hovels, settled and well watered in scattered groups: Cromford itself at the junction of Bonsall Dale with the Roman Hereward Street, the smaller hamlet of Scarthin across Bonsall Brook and a settlement out of view behind a rock called Willersley. By all accounts, Willersley, now lost, was an attractive little village, sitting on the bank of the river Derwent, where fishing was, and still is, good.

The hillsides would have been mostly bare of trees for they had mostly been cut by the miner for smelting his lead. A pall of acrid and poisonous smoke would have hung in the valley on a calm day from the smelter at Willersley and another in Bonsall Dale. Cromford Moor would have suffered from the emissions from a smelter at Steeple House. Transport would have been on foot for most, on horse back for the better off and by coach for the rich. There would have been a brisk traffic through the village of Cromford from and to Wirksworth, then the second most important town in the county. Coaches and wagons would rattle down the hill from Cromford Moor and struggle back up with sweating and panting horses.

A sketch entitled "A view of Cromford, Matlock Bath". It is more likely to be a view of Willersley with a few of the cottages and a smelter in the middle distance. Arkwrights "castle" would be built to the left of the view. c1750.
(Derbyshire County Library)

To access Matlock meant a walk over the hills via Bonsall on the west or the climb over Starkholmes to the east. This latter journey would have meant crossing an ancient bridge, before ascending Willersley Lane. Before this bridge was built in the 15th century, travellers would have had to cross the river by a ford, immediately downstream from the bridge of today. To help these travellers on their journeys, a bridge chapel ensured their spiritual welfare and a squint in a wall holding a light, ensured that they did not go astray in the water on a dark night. This must have been a hazardous crossing to warrant such measures, one can understand this when watching the river in spate after the snows have melted on the moors.

The occupants would have walked to church in Wirksworth for Sunday service, to bury their dead, to baptise their children and to marry, although there is a tradition that a church stood where St Mary's now stands many years ago. They would have trod the same route to go to market, not only to buy but to sell any surplus produce of their own. Medicine was from home made remedies, childbirth was attended to by unskilled women who also laid out the dead. Some may have ventured to Matlock to attend the market there, but this would have been no better than the one at Wirksworth.

They ate oat cakes, still made and sold in the village, for in those days oats was a staple crop in the thin soil of these hills, as was mutton, lamb as we know it was not eaten in those times. Of sheep there were many, for the hillsides would have been swarming with them. English wool still fetched a good price and was favoured by the weavers on the continent. A few cows were kept on the lowland pastures such as Cromford Meadows for their milk, which would be made into cheese for winter consumption. Each hovel would have its pig, which would be ritually slaughtered in Autumn and the sides hung in the smoke filled hovel to cure, a good pig ate waste and produced enough bacon for the family to see them through winter, nothing being left apart from its squeal. A few chickens might be kept for their eggs and towards the end of their miserable lives, they would have their necks "rung" and become a rare delicacy on the table.

There would have been little noise, no motor vehicles or trains, just the bleating of sheep, the lowing of the cows, the shouts amongst the villagers and the clink of the blacksmith at his anvil. This would have been largely a self sufficient community, having a cordwainer, rope maker, a wise woman (who delivered babies, laid out the dead and made up concoctions as cure-alls) and butcher as well as the smith, who would undertake to shoe a horse, make a drill for a miner and repair a plough for the farmer.

Mining would have been the most significant activity in the parish. They sought the lead and zinc to be found in the veins in the hillsides, veins having strange names such as rakes, scrins and pipes with exotic titles such as Bullestree Pasture Vein, Moletrap Vein, Alabaster Vein, Hallicar Vein, Rose Rake, Carnel Level. They would also have been aware that there were several soughs, or drainage tunnels driven into the hillside, which emitted water at all times of the year, some of it steaming as a reminder of the depths they penetrated, these too had exotic names: Carnhill, Wives Sough, Bates Sough, Vermuydens Sough.

Some of the terms used by the miner from his unique and broad vocabulary are still in use today amongst the older residents: the waste from a sink is a sough, the gutter round the eaves is a launder, poisoned land is belland. Mining is in their blood and for centuries it has carried on from father to son either as a full time occupation or as an additional form of income to farming or inn-keeping.

The area comes under the administrative district of the Soke, Wapentake and Hundred of Wirksworth, which area is also the King's Field for lead mining purposes. The unique Mineral Courts Act for Derbyshire of 1851 and 1852 ratified the better customs held since time without memory, administered by the oldest industrial court in the world held in the Moot Hall, Wirksworth. The act guarantees that any person can search for and dig for lead in Derbyshire without let or hindrance, with certain sensible exclusions. Whilst the industry is now dead, the court still sits and conducts business. This system has been of enormous value to the ordinary miner for it allowed him to dig and operate his own mine with only a limited amount of capital. This is how the miners operated in Cromford for centuries, and the names found in the Barmaster's records dating back several hundreds of years are the same names which are found in the village today. The evidence of lead mining surrounds the area and intrudes into the village.

Quarrying was and is a significant industry, for limestone for making lime and for road making and millstone for grinding corn and building stone. The millstone is found over the limestone with a deep bed of shale between them, forming an impervious layer. This layer collects the water soaking down from the moors and produces a series of springs. It is this shale which was exploited for the easy driving of the soughs and which is causing concern today as this is the source of Radon gas.

To the traveller then, the area must have seemed a bleak and inhospitable place, a place which could not be traversed in any direction without having to ford streams, scale steep hills, with muddy roads and always an overcoat colder than anywhere else.

The village sits on marginal land, the interface between the richer pastures of the alluvial valley bottom, made better by the silt brought down during the long life of the river Derwent, the lower hillside which sits on limestone, where the grazing is good and in stark contrast the acidic uplands where the moors support some sheep, grouse, heather and bilberry. The burning of limestone would have been important, for having produced quicklime, the burner would add water to slake it and the farmers would spread it on the acid soils so as to neutralise them. Eventually good eating grass would replace the heather and a little more land was won for agriculture. The effects can be seen when the liming is neglected, for the moorland plants soon encroach again.

It was to this scene that Arkwright first saw the village when he was out buying hair from the women, when he was a wig maker in Bolton in the county Palatine of Lancaster. Of all the places he saw, Cromford seemed to appeal to him most, for he found people who were already using stocking frames, plenty of water and cheap labour, men and women who were anxious to get regular wages and work in a warm environment. He was a man of vision, and he shared the same vision of other self-made men of that period, men such as Josiah Wedgwood in Burslem, Staffordshire who was similar to Arkwright in so many ways.

Had Arkwright not chosen Cromford for his new ideas, what would it have become? Possibly it would have been caught up in the boom in hydropathy which came on Arkwright's heels, perhaps instead of the mills we would have had a hospital type of establishment? It is easy to speculate, perhaps with hindsight we prefer what Arkwright did!

He left us with a well planned village having a pleasing aspect. His industry has created a new industry of nostalgia, for the village attracts hundreds of visitors each year to see what Arkwright did, most of these are school children doing projects, some are historians and foreign languages are often witnessed amongst the visitors.

To some extent, the village has become a dormitory for people who work in Chesterfield, Sheffield and Nottingham. Some years ago a man travelled daily to Coventry to work in a car plant. Significantly, many retired people, mostly from the south, have retired to Cromford, a southern accent, which sounds "posh" to the natives, is common in the shops.
Some of the residents have made their names elsewhere in the world and one such instance forms part of chapter eight.

We owe Arkwright other debts. His desire for a fine landscape to view from his new house coupled with his love of trees has meant that what was a barren area, is now green with numerous trees, predominantly deciduous, a source of great enjoyment to us all. The area is laced with pleasant walks ranging from hard to easy. If he had not been here we would not have had the Cromford and High Peak Railway, which means that we would not have that superb amenity, the High Peak Trail, a traffic free access which climbs hills and crosses fields without passing through a single town or village. It links with the Tissington Trail to provide a network of access routes for the walker, cyclist and horse rider.

Without him we would not have had the canal tow path to walk along, and what a joy that is to the naturalist, with its birds, voles, bats, snakes and flowers. We would not have the mill pond in the centre of the village either with its trout, swans and kingfishers.

During the Arkwright family's period as Lords of the manor, there was a rash of building, for as well as the housing, the chapel goer was provided for as well as the church goer. Alas, of the six original places of worship, only St Mary's church and the Methodist Church survive as places of worship, the others have been given over to a car repair shop, an engineering business and a private house. The Glenorchy Chapel has gone to make way for road widening..

It is a place of views, for anyone can access the summit of the Black Rocks, Masson Hill and Bilberry Knoll - this latter on private land - to have a bird's eye panorama of the village and its environs. One would be struck by the scars of quarrying which have grown significantly over the last thirty years but one would also be pleased with the sight of the mature trees and the crags. This is romantic scenery of the highest order and it attracts many people, mostly day visitors, who find the car park at the Black Rocks, to be a convenient setting off point for walking or cycling on the High Peak Trail.

Those of us who live here love this village and its history and we would not live anywhere else!

The Mill Pond with Scarthin on the left. circa 1900

Chapter Two
The Romans, the Normans and beyond

Village histories usually start with either the Romans or the Normans - this history will be no different. We have little to go on for the earlier history of our villages, for prehistory we rely on artefacts rather than the written word.

> But the Romans came with a heavy hand,
>   And bridged and roaded and ruled the land,
> And the Romans left and the Danes blew in -
>   And that's where our history-books begin.
>   Rudyard Kipling, *The River's Tale*, 1911

The Romans were certainly active in the area. They have left us with Hereward Street which runs through the village and they left some artefacts, the chief of which are pigs of lead, found in the parish and inscribed in abbreviated Latin. There are numerous pigs of Roman origin in existence from the Derbyshire mining field but we will concentrate on those found locally.

Two pigs found in the churchyard in 1918 and almost identical are inscribed XXX and XV and weigh 112 lb (51 kg). A pig was found on Cromford Moor in 1777 which has a more revealing inscription:

> IMP. CAES. HADRIANI. AUG. MET. LVT.

This translated gives us: Emperor Caesar Hadrian Augustus Metalorum Lutudarum. This inscription in varying forms has been found on several other pigs found in and out of the county. As it was a tribute for Hadrian, it must have dated between 117 and 138 AD. The reference to Lutudarum has been a mystery for many years it having been ascribed to various places including Matlock, Wirksworth, Chesterfield, Church Wilne (incredibly) or to a mining "field", perhaps influenced by the Saxon establishment of such fields as the King's Field for the Soke and Wapentake of Wirksworth. During excavations before Carsington Water flooded the Henmore Valley, it was established that a settlement found there is most probably the long sought after Lutudarum. This place is also at the crossing of the two Roman roads, Hereward Street and the Street, the latter being the road from Little Chester (Derventio) to Buxton (Aqua Arnametiae). Also in the Ravennas it is listed as a place, possibly a Roman station, second only in importance to Derventio. This latter is now covered by Little Chester, a suburb of Derby.

On analysis, this pig produced 1 oz 19.5 dwts (30 grammes) per ton (1017 kg) of lead. Derbyshire lead has always been argentiferous and this is a small figure. Lead from Goodluck Mine in the Via Gellia revealed 17 ozs/ton, Ball Eye Mine also on the Via Gellia produced 22 oz/ton, this latter being considered a record for the county. This inscription suggests that the lead might have been de-silvered at the smelter, the metalorum.

Other evidence of the Romans in the area is perhaps more exciting:

- a Roman coin discovered near Gardens at the roadside of Cromford Hill in the 1950s. It was of a copper/silver alloy and minted in Constantinople (today's Istanbul). It was inscribed:

FEL. TEMP. REPARATIO-FEL(ICIUM) TEMP(ORUM) REPERATIO

translated as "a return to secure and happier times". This coin is of the period of Constantine II (349-50 AD)

- a skeleton with over 60 Roman coins was found near Bonsall Hollow, 900 yards West of Cromford Meadows. This is probably the find referred to as having been found when Scarthin Nick was cut. The coins were small and of copper of the time of Licinius and Constantine (4th Century AD).

- whilst outside our area but close to it was found a much worn yellowish freestone during excavations at Ibet Low near Hopton in 1796 by a Mr. H Rooke. The damaged inscription read:

GELL....
PRAE CO III
L.V. BRIT.

It was this stone found on Gell land that inspired the Gells to believe that not only were they descended from a Roman but had occupied the same area for nearly two millennia. The L.V. is of interest for it looks like a reference to Lutudarum, the BRIT may be a reference to the local tribe of Brittones or Brigantes. Our area falls inside the area known as Brigantia.

What further treasures await discovery? Time will tell. There is sufficient to confirm that the Romans were in the area and probably worked the mines for lead on a tribute system, whereby the local indigenous people produced the lead in return for food and protection. The Roman presence was only token for all the work was done by others. Of these Romans it has been found that many in the county were mercenaries from Spain. How they must have longed for Iberia when the snow was falling and the north wind blowing!

The Saxon influence is to be found in the traditions of lead mining which are unique to Derbyshire. The Barmote Court still sits at the Moot Hall at Wirksworth where all matters covering the mining of lead are judged. The proceedings are carried out by a Steward and the senior officer is a Barmaster from the Old Saxon for Bergermiester. Similar courts are recorded as taking place in Saxony.

Of several invaders, the Danes were one of the few who settled in the area. By 876, Cromford was part of Danish Mercia and came under the Danelaw. Derby along with Nottingham, Leicester, Stamford and Lincoln was one of the five Danish boroughs. In the crypt of St. Wystan's church at Repton is a mausoleum for the Mercian kings in use during the 8th and 9th centuries.. At this time, Cromford also came under the Bishopric of Lichfield, which pertained until 1927 when the diocese of Derby was created.

The Normans arrived, as every school child will tell us in 1066 and the greatest document from this period is the much lauded Domesday Survey. In this we will find that Cromford was spelled Crunforde meaning a ford by a bend of a river, being ascribed to the Derwent by scholars. One could take issue with this for a bend in the Bonsall Brook which was actually in the village - not underground as it now is - is a more sensible attribution, the ford being the one that traversed this brook when going to Bonsall. The bend in the Derwent belongs to Willersley more than Cromford. Cromford at that time, 1086, was a berewic or outlier of the manor of Wirksworth along with Middleton 2c, Hopton 4c, Welledene 2C, Carsington 2C, Callow 2C, (Kirk) Ireton 4c. The c stands for carucate, of which Cromford had 2. A carucate (carucata) is a measure of land found in Danish areas and is equal to 8 Bovates (Bovata). The survey lists three lead works (iii. Plumbariae) at Wirksworth, these probably being lead smelting works rather than lead mines. In those times lead was smelted in boles and we have Bole Hill overlooking the village. Welledene is an outlier that has never been found - the writer believes it to be Wigwell on Wirksworth Moor where there is evidence of ancient settlement round Moor Farm and Wigwell Grange.

In the year of the survey, Wirksworth and its outliers was Terra Regis, the land of the King. Along with four others manors - Darley, Matlock (Bridge), Ashbourne and Parwich - Wirksworth and its outliers paid tax in the form of pure silver valued at £40. This considerable sum is an indicator that the lead was being mined in sufficient quantities to produce large amounts of silver The reference to pure silver is of interest for it suggests that by this date refining techniques were improving. The same area before the conquest was producing £32 in payment and 6.5 sesters of honey. This latter indicates that the area must have been known for its apiculture, a rare reference in Domesday. The Lord who enjoyed this income before William was Leofric in 1045 and Edwin prior to 1066.

The area is heavily planted with trees, most being planted by the Arkwrights in the nineteenth century. At the time of the Conqueror, the Royal Forest of Duffield, the Duffield Frith extended this far. The Frith would have been out of bounds for ordinary folk on pain of death, a stray dog forfeited its paws, a man lost his sight if he were lucky. It has been calculated that 26% of Derbyshire was wooded in 1086. William who enjoyed Terra Regis should have been known as William the Terror. His harrying of the north had a marginal effect on Cromford.

In 1350, Edward III (reigned 1327-77) granted the right of free warren in Cromford to Sir Hugh de Meynell of Meynell Langley. Sir Hugh died in 1364 seized of the manor, held under the Duke of Lancaster. This reference to warren is of interest for it was a term applied to enclosures for the raising of deer or rabbits. Rabbits were introduced from Iberia and the Balearic Islands as a culinary delicacy and were a rich crop. Warrens had to be created for them to protect them from predators and holes dug for them for shelter for these rabbits did not know how to burrow having come from countries where life on the surface was comfortable. This warrening was almost certainly for rabbits and it established a tradition of hat making in Cromford which was strong in the nineteenth century.

Those who held the manor were as follows:

- 1066   Edward the Confessor
- 1086   Terra Regis - William the Conqueror
- 1350   Edward III granted the right of free warren to Sir Hugh de Meynell of Meynell Langley
- 1364   Sir Hugh died seized of the manor under the Duke of Lancaster
- Henry VI c.1450   Richard Minors conveyed the manor to Sir Roger Leche -
- Henry VIII   Leche family sold to the Agard family
- 1548   Thomas Agard died seized of the manor
- 1556   Purchased from the Agards (along with Chatsworth) by Sir William Cavendish, second husband of Bess of Hardwick, Bess's fourth husband -Gilbert Talbot, Earl of Shrewsbury conveyed the manor to his son Henry Talbot, his youngest son and Bess's step-son, of Ronalton, Nottinghamshire
- 1595   Henry Talbot died seized of the manor
- 1596   Henry's daughter and co-heiress, Lady Armine (Dame Mary Talbot). held the manor. She built and endowed the Bede Houses in Cromford in 1654.

The manor then passed by natural descent to:
> her daughter and co-heiress Gertrude who married Robert Pierrepoint, later Duke of Kingston.

- in a family settlement it went to William Pierrepoint of a cadet branch of the family
- it was bequeathed to his widow a co-heiress of Sir Thomas Darcy Bt. who died childless
- settled on her nephew Sir Darcy Dawes Bt. son of Archbishop Dawes
- Sir Darcy's daughter and heiress left it to Edwin Lascelles later to be Lord Harewood

1716	Bought by William Soresby William Soresby, grandson of the above died unmarried, his two sisters became co-heiresses. The two heiresses married: Mary to William Milnes and Helen to the Reverend Thomas Munro. Milnes bought Munro's moeity
1776	Sold to Peter Nightingale of Lea
1789	Sold to Richard, later Sir Richard, Arkwright who also bought the manor of Willersley from Thomas Hallett Hodges.

The Nightingale family who bought the manor of Willersley in 1778 is the same family as the founder of modern nursing, Florence Nightingale, who lived part of her life at Lea Hurst and used the income from the estate to start her work at Scutari in the Crimea. The Nightingales sold the manor to Arkwright in 1789 who also bought the manor of Willersley.

It is clear that at this time Willersley was larger than Cromford and a pleasant sort of settlement. It boasted a smelter and an inn where the gates now stand on the Matlock road. The evidence is scant but could be worse.

We all wait with hope that some great find will be made to cast new light on the early history of Cromford, for given its importance as a river crossing it must have been well used. There is evidence that a church once stood where today's St. Mary's church now stands. This later church was built where a lead smelter stood.

The village changed its name over the centuries from the Cruneforde of the Domesday Survey to Crumford and finally Cromford. Significantly some of the older villagers years ago referred to the village as Crumford.

Up to the time of Arkwright the village would have remained little changed with its adjoining hamlets of Scarthin and Willersley. The dramatic changes wrought by Arkwright must have taken everybody by surprise. The clearing of hovels and the build ing of his workers' housing, the Greyhound Hotel, the mills, church and his mansion, Willersley Castle. The village would have benefited by all this with improvements in diet bought by regular wages and the availability of better housing and medicine.

It is difficult for us today to envisage how it all looked before his time with the Bonsall Brook running through the village and the muddy (or dusty) roads running through to Wirksworth. Having to walk to Wirksworth to go to church, not only to worship but to get married, to baptise ones children and for the funeral rites. The nearest doctor and market were also at Wirksworth. The village would have had to endure shifts in fortune based on the price of lead. In good times when the price was good they enjoyed a degree of prosperity, at other times they suffered hunger and deprivation. All this ended with Arkwright.

Before his arrival life was brutish and short. He created a community which was the envy of others and was copied many times. We are fortunate that his Cromford is largely still with us.

This View of WILLERSLEY CASTLE, in Matlock is most respectfully dedicated to Richard Arkwright Esq. by his obliged humble Servant, Stephen Glover.

Chapter Three
Mining

"a rude boorish kind of people - who they call Peakrills, who work in the mines"
"bold, daring and even desperate kind of fellows . . . . who search into the bowels of the earth"

Daniel Defoe, 1726

The mining of lead was the mainstay economy of Cromford before the arrival of the cotton spinning mills. However we must not forget the other minerals mined in the parish and often in the same mines: calamine, zinc and pigments. We have no record of mining in the parish until recently, but it is undoubted that men were mining for lead under the Romans and later. Two pigs of Roman lead found in the parish are referred to in chapter two.

Cromford is one of the Liberties forming the mining "field" known as the King's Field, which comprises the Soke, Wapentake and Hundred of Wirksworth. The mining customs enshrined in the Derbyshire Mineral Courts Act of 1852 apply to Cromford and any disputes arising over the mining of lead must be dealt with by the Great Barmote Court which still sits each year in the Moot Hall at Wirksworth. The lessee of the duties is the Duke of Devonshire, the Lord of the Field is H.M. Queen Elizabeth in her right as the Duke of Lancaster. The current Barmaster is William Erskine and the Steward, Michael Cockerton both of Bakewell.

The story of lead mining in Cromford is very much the story of the miners' battle with water. Lead veins (or rakes, scrins or pipes as they are called locally) occur in the area and the rakes, the stronger veins, are vertical or nearly so. These rakes were pursued downwards by the miner until the water table prevented further exploitation, where-upon he pumped the water out using primitive methods such as hand bailing, rag and chain pumps and waterwheels. There comes a time when these no longer succeed and a new device was tried, the sough (pronounced 'suff').

The earliest record of lead production in the area, Roman apart, dates from 714 when the mines were paying dues to the Nunnery at Repton in south Derbyshire, the Abbess in that year sent a lead sarcophagus to Croyland in Lincolnshire for the burial of St. Guthlas, formerly a monk at Repton. In 835, Abbess Kenewara granted the mines to Aeldorman Humberht, the rent for the mines being 300 shillings' worth of lead for Christ Church, Canterbury to the account of Archbishop Ceolnoth. There could be lead from Cromford in the roof of Canterbury Cathedral which is over 1100 years old.

When the Danes destroyed the religious houses in the 9th century it would appear that these mines reverted to the crown, possibly in 874 when the Nunnery at Repton was sacked by a raiding-party. We then have a large gap in our knowledge, probably because there was little if any activity in the mining field. The next record is dated

1469, when whilst under the reign of Edward IV all mineral duties north of the River Trent were leased to Richard, Earl of Northumberland and others for 40 years. The ever active Elizabeth I granted the lease to Messrs. Warren and Skelton, James I, who was equally active, leased them to Gilbert, Earl of Shrewsbury - one of the husbands of Bess of Hardwick - in 1609. The same monarch then leased them to a Robert Parker for 31 years at a rent of £72 per annum with £1.6s.8d (£1.33) to the Barmaster. This was in 1624 and the lease should have expired in 1655 but after eleven years, for reasons unknown, but possible failure to pay the rent, the lease was taken over by a David Ramsay for a period of 31 years. After the interregnum, Charles II gave the lease to George Vernon, of Haddon for seven years at a rent of £144 for lot and cope, with £2.13s.4d (£2.66) for the Barmaster. On the death of Charles, the mines became part of the dowry of the Dowager Queen Catherine, who leased the lot and cope to a Robert Freeman for 31 years from 5th March, 1692 in her right as the Duke of Lancaster.

This Duchy was annexed by Edward IV, our present Queen is the Duke - not Duchess - of Lancaster. As the crown owned the mineral dutes outright in their right as Earls and Dukes of Lancaster, they had jure regalia (Royal law), having the same prerogatives in the Courts Palatine and in the Duchy as in lands held jure coronae (Crown law). The Moot Hall in Wirksworth is the property of the Queen's Lancaster Estates, falling under the Crewe Survey. The toasts taken to Her Majesty at the Barmote dinner are in her name as the Duke of Lancaster as are the functions of the court.

Robert Freeman assigned a third of his lease to Chief Baron Montague. In 1733, Elizabeth Lady Dowager Clifford of Chudleigh, Devonshire, widow of Hugh, Lord Clifford, was seized of two thirds of the mineral due and the office of Barmaster. These she granted to Denzil, Lord Holles and other trustees of Queen Catharine who in turn leased them to a mixed group of men:

>   Richard Milnes of Chesterfield, grocer
>   James Milnes (the younger) of Chesterfield, merchant,
>   Joshua Wheeldon of Chesterfield, distiller
>   John Wall of Wensley, Gent
>   Wyley Hayward of Cromford, lead merchant
>   Robert Matlock of Derby, writing-master

for three years from 25th March, 1733, the rent being £433.6s.8d (£433.33) per annum.

In 1753 the lease was taken by a Mr. Rolls and in 1809 Richard Arkwright bought the remainder of Holles's lease and they remained with the Arkwright family until they passed to the Dukes of Devonshire as farmers of the lead where they remain to this day.
The duties of lot and cope were leased by the owner of the mineral field, of late the Duchy of Lancaster. The Barmaster was responsible for collecting these dues for the

farmer, and they comprised every 19th dish of ore for lot and a fee levied on every load bought for cope. Also until the last century, a tithe was paid on lead ore as it was believed that the ore grew. Tithes were exercised on anything which grew and were payable to the church, hence the fine church at Wirkwsorth, built on the strength of mining.

Cromford can boast the earliest sough driven in Derbyshire and it was pioneered by a Dutchman, one Cornelius Vermuyden, later made Sir Cornelius in recognition of the work he did draining Hatfield Chase in North Lincolnshire. The theory behind driving soughs is simple, the digging of them not so. They chose a point down valley from the drowned rake and commenced tunnelling at a slight slope upwards, a near horizontal tunnel, until it met the rake, when the rake would drain down the sough and out to the surface.

Several soughs were driven into the hillside of Cromford which climbs up to the top of the road to 'Wirksworth. The hill top is of Millstone Grit, the lower slopes of Limestone with a band of shale separating them. The earlier soughs followed this band of shale, for it made digging easier. The rakes to which these soughs were aimed ran in the hillside and had been exploited from the hill top. The map in this section indicates the stronger of these rakes, there were many more lesser ones.

The stronger rakes were named eloquently after the name of the first person to free or mine the vein, in optimism of its productivity, or after local features. The following is far from being a comprehensive list:

- Godbehere's Founder - Godbehere (Godber today) was a local family. A founder is a mine which has been established by due legal process and forms the original working, in this case a shaft.
- Tinley Vein (yes they also called them veins) now famous for being the site of the earliest use of gunpowder for mining in Britain.
- Sliding Pits Vein - suggests that the vein had a hade - or inclination - which caused people or loose matter to slide on the wet surface.
- Gretorex Vein - the Greatorex's were and still are a local family.
- Dragon Eye Vein - named for a characteristic within the mine
- Alabaster Vein - because alabaster - a fine form of gypsum ($CaSO_4.2H_2O$) - was found here. This occurrence is unusual in the area - it being common in the south of the county especially in Chellaston - a deposit was also found as Selenite in Cumberland Cavern, Matlock Bath.
- Moletrap Vein - because it had the characteristics of a mole-run with traps.
- Bullstree Pasture Vein - a corruption of Bullace Tree, one assumes such a tree once grew here.

Of the soughs - again see the map - several are now lost through their entrances being collapsed or covered with spoil, etc. The following is a more comprehensive list, for much is now known about them:

- Vermuydens Sough (1629-36) - the original one driven by the Dutchman, Sir Cornelius Vermuyden of Grays Inn, London, the son of a Dutch engineer. The portal is now lost but was at GR 294 566, now covered with the quarry embankments - Dean Quarry on Cromford Hill. Whilst the work was under way, Vermuyden leased the ore from Dovegang Mine whilst driving this sough in 1637. By 1651 there was a waterwheel, there were two here in 1800 with a third by 1815 which raised water from 60 feet below sough level, these had fly-wheels and pendulum pumps.

- Bates Sough - portal collapsed but recognisable as a spring near to the Bede Houses.

- Alabaster Sough, as its name implies drains the Alabaster Mine, the portal is in the mill race of the mill on Water Lane.

- Cromford Sough or Long or Longhead Sough (1673-82) - an epic story lies behind the digging of this famous sough. Its portal can be seen with a little water issuing from it in the Bear Pit, behind the shops on Cromford Hill. The original portal exited into the Bonsall Brook in the Market Place. It is this sough which excited Arkwright in his search for a reliable source of water. It is a little thermal and the water emits steam on a frosty day. The miners followed the boundary of the shale to make the work less arduous. This must have had its dangers as the shale gives off methane gas, which would have been a danger as the miners used candles for illumination. Surprisingly there is no record of explosions. Ventilation was bad and a relief tunnel had to be dug parallel with the sough, connecting to the Roggelim Shaft, at the bottom of which was a fire basket to encourage air flow. This method was borrowed from coal mines and must have been exceedingly dangerous in a gaseous mine. When completed, this sough led to greater prosperity in the mines it drained, based on the Godbehere Vein, also branches of the sough known as: the Bedehouse Branch, Tinley Vein, Dragon Eye Vein and Gretorex Vein.

The driving of the Meerbrook Sough, portal near Whatstandwell, which drained the mines in the Wirksworth basin and Cromford Hill to a depth deeper by forty feet, which caused the Cromford soughs to almost dry up. Peter Arkwright defended his right to the water from Cromford Sough but lost his case. At noon, on 21st September, 1844 work stopped at the Cromford mills through lack of water brought about by the loss of sough water, the first time this had ever happened. The original of this sough took from 1772 to 1811 to drive at a cost of £45,000 (about £45 million today). It was carried as far as Bolehill and unwatered the veins above Cromford to a lower level than the soughs in the parish. A further extension by a new company (1840-46) costing £70,000 (£70 million today) put the final nail in the coffin of water powered spinning. The Cromford Sough was and still is rendered dry and in 1837 its effect was felt on the mills, the upper mill closing in 1846. After a court case against the Arkwright family, the mills were as good as finished. The Meerbrook Sough was bought by the Ilkeston and Heanor Water Board later part of the South Derbyshire Water Board, who used part of the water, the rest joining the river Derwent nearby. It now forms part of Severn Trent Water. Its five miles – with branches – discharges 17 million gallons of water a day (77.3 million litres per day). The large stone portal has the initials F.H.1772 inscribed upon it, to commemorate the principal proprietor of that time, Francis Hurt.

The mine referred to above, Godbehere's Founder was the scene of considerable drama in 1797, when two miners, Job Boden and Anthony Pearson, were inundated with mud and water which ran into the mine to a depth of fifty-four yards. Their colleagues dug furiously until on the third day they found Pearson dead in an upright position. After a further eight days they found Boden alive albeit dehydrated and emaciated. However, after a rest of fourteen weeks he was well enough to resume work in the mine. There is evidence, albeit brief, that there was a steam engine on this vein in the 1920s, possibly left over from the installation of a steam whimsey of 1818 of which the chimney stump at Black Rocks picnic site is a remnant.

Tinley Vein was at one time, along with others called Dun Rake, Rose Rake, Ashbrook Rake, was owned by no less than sixty-one persons in 1676, one of whom was Sir John Gell of Hopton Hall. As well as a Doctor of Divinity of London and a Bachelor of Divinity of Magdalen College, Cambridge. Such was the diversity of ownership at that time.

Cromford (or Long) Sough was also famous for the discovery of a supposed new mineral, appropriately named Cromfordite. This mineral is now rare and the first record of its discovery is from the 1780s. It was also found in mines unwatered by this sough in the adjoining liberty known as Bage Mine and Wall Close Vein, both in Bolehill. Cromfordite is a close relative of another rare mineral also found nearby called Matlockite ($PbFCl$), both being forms of Phosgenite ($Pb_2(CO_3)Cl_2$). There are specimens in some museums including the British Museum and private collections.

The smelting of the lead ore - galena, a sulphide of lead - was undertaken originally in bole furnaces located on hillsides, hence Bolehill which overlooks the village from the west. Later furnaces were located at Steeple House where the new Wirksworth Cemetery now stands and by Cromford Bridge on an area known as The Green. This latter one was in use when Arkwright arrived and it was this site which he chose for his church of St. Mary. The Nightingale family were well known lead smelters in this area and this smelter was probably one of theirs when they owned the estate.
Its bellows were driven by a water wheel located in the river Derwent, fifty yards

upstream from the church. This wheel drew water from above a weir, the eighth on this river between Matlock Bridge and Cromford Bridge of which seven drove pumps for draining lead mines. The village of Willersley existed to service this smelter all of which was cleared by Arkwright as it came into view from his new "castle".

There were other minerals found in the Cromford mines, alabaster and forms of phosgenite have already been mentioned. Others, most of which were a form of added income to the miners were:

- calamine, an oxide of zinc which was used medicinally and as an additive to quicklime to make cement was also an important ore of zinc metal, an important constituent for brass making. The calamine-lime mix was used by Arkwright as a mortar when building his mills. After roasting it makes zinc metal. 500 tons per annum was produced in the parish along with Wirksworth. The Cheadle Brass and Copper Company built in the 1720s the original mill which stood here. Arkwright demolished most of it to make way for his corn mill. The Cheadle company imported smelters from their works at Cheadle, near Uttoxeter, Staffordshire and housed them in a row of houses built for the purpose, known today as Staffordshire Row (these were not built by Arkwright for cotton spinners from Staffordshire as commonly believed, they were built before he was born, circa 1720). Most of their calamine came from Bonsall Moor and the resulting zinc metal was carried by packhorse to the foundry at Cheadle, where it was melted down, mixed with copper from Ecton Hill and elsewhere, and made into brass. The same mill also ground the calamine prior to roasting.

- blende or blackjack sometimes known as mock lead, was also used for the manufacture of brass. This along with calamine was sold to the Birmingham Brass Foundry Company who had a warehouse in the village.

- barytes, used as a base for paint and lately as a slurry for the drilling for oil in the North Sea.

- pyrites

- manganese

- fluorspar of several colours but not of "Blue John" quality.

- ochre of several colours used locally by pigment and paint manufacturers, of which there was one in the Via Gellia (Taylors) and one in the village where the water wheel now revolves. This mill was used by one of the Wheatcroft family, Henry, who at the turn of the century was grinding, "blacks, ivory, blue and mineral, chromates, blue vermillionettes and numerous others." Most of these earths were from the local mines and Wheatcroft was one of the largest producers in the county. He also produced lead oxide or minium, much sought after for preserving ironwork on bridges and the like.

In the catalogue of the Great Exhibition of 1851, *Volume I- Class 1- Mining and Mineral Products,* item 87 records "Specimens of fluorspar, calcareous spar, calamine, white lead ore, lead ore, sulphate of barytes, and sulphate of barytes manufactured as a pigment, From the Dinah, Goodluck and other mines in the vicinity of Cromford". These were from William Potter and Company, 87, Aldgate, London and with a warehouse in Cromford. The Goodluck Mine referred to is not the one in the Via Gellia in the Liberty of Middleton-by-Wirksworth but the Goodluck Vein on Bolehill.

Cromford Moor Mine c. 1800
This shows a horse gin and the Black Rocks

*Old sough portal, originally the water supply on North Street.
(P.J. Naylor)*

*Lead Miners' Trials. Allen Hill
(author)*

Map of the soughs and veins in the Liberty of Cromford

Minor veins, scrins, etc are not shown for clarity

Based on earlier maps by:

1923 Cromford sough dialled by William and Thomas Hodson
1974 Freeings 15th Aspril 1698 to 21st May 1714 by Roger Flindall
1982 Survey of Cromford Sough by R P Shaw and J D Harrison
1987 History and Gazetteer of Lead Mine Soughs of Derbyshire
   by Dr J H Rieuwerts - Private publication.

Plotted on a map of 1841 (Courtesy Derbyshire Record Office)

SOUGHS

CS	Cromford Sough (Fern Sough, Long Sough, Cromford Moor Sough, Roggelim Sough)
CSP	Cromford Sough, Portal- original location now lost
CS.BP	Cromford Sough, present portal in the Bear Pit
CS.RL	Cromford Sough, relief level.
CS.RL.P	Cromford Sough, relief level portal
CS.OF	Cromford Sough, overflow levels, two total
CS.S	Cromford Sough, shaft to "day"
CS.MPS	Milking Place Shaft (or Boarded Coe Shaft)
CS.RS	Rogelim Shaft, which had the fire basket
CS.BHB	Cromford Sough, Bede Houses branch
CS.GB	Cromford Sough, Greatorex branch
CS.HC	Cromford Sough, hard cut (bye-pass of 1742)
CS.PG	Parallel gates for ventilation, 1706-9

A section of 1815 shows three water wheels and two pendulum pumps with fly-wheels in this sough

BS	Bates Sough (Longhead Sough, Loosey Sough, Cromford Moor Sough) driven 1657-c.1684
BS.P	Bates Sough portal (now lost)
BS.P?	Bates Sough portal (possible alternative)
VS	Vermuyden's Sough (Dutchmans's Level, Gang Sough) Driven 1631-1651
SPVS	Sliding Pits Vein Sough
SVS	Vein Sough portal
AS	Alabaster Sough
AS.P	Alabaster Sough portal in the mill race

Other veins and other features

ACV	Ashcross Vein
CMM	Cromford Moor Mine, now capped – Black Rocks car park
BV	Barrow Vein
CS	Chapman Scrin
DB	Dean Bottom (The Dean or Dene is where the quarry now is)
DNS	Dove Nest Shaft
DEV	Dragon Eye Vein
SVES	Shore Vein Engine Shaft
DR	Dun Rake
GBV	Godbehere's vein (Godber's Vein) – a local family
GHV	Greyhound Vein (The greyhound is the crest on the Gell family arms)
GTV	Gaunt's Vein (local family)
GV	Gang Vein
HG	Horse Gate
HPV	Honey Pot Vein
HWV	Henry Wigton's Venture (local family)
OV	Oldfield Vein (a prominent local family)
RR	Rose Rake or Great Rose Rake Vein
SBV	Stony Butts Vein
SPV	Sliding Pitts Vein
STV	Sling Tor (Slinter) Tor Vein (near to Slinter Tor and Wood)
TEV	Tail Edge Vein
TV	Tinley Vein
VV	Venture Vein
WLV	Wragg's Little Vein (local family)
WGV	Wragg's Great Vein (local family)

Map of the soughs and veins in the Liberty of Cromford

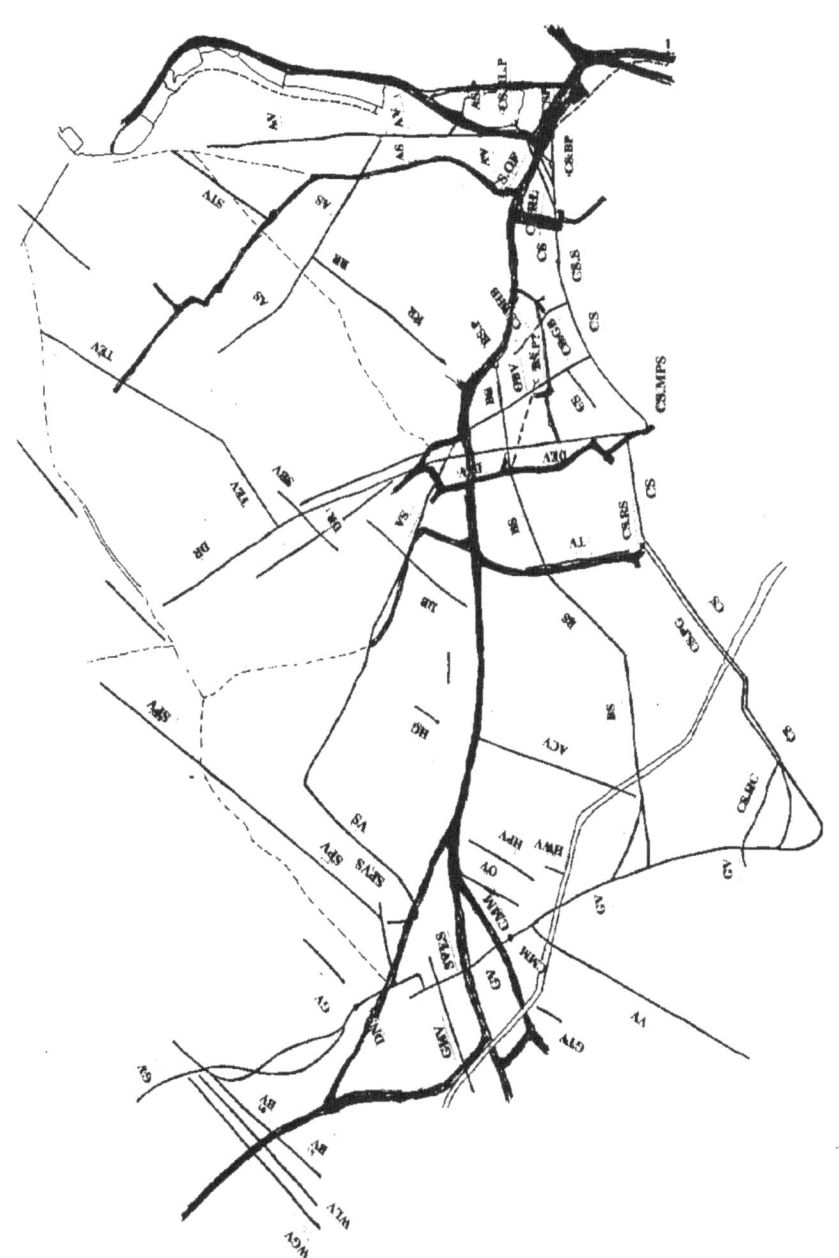

The "Bear Pit" - two outlets, one to the Mill Pond, the other to the brook under the Market Place *(Author)*

Chapter Four
The Age of Arkwright

Note:
All references to "Arkwright" in this chapter are meant to be Sir Richard and not his son Richard, who is referred to as Richard Junior or Jnr.

> So Arkwright taught from cotton buds to cull
>   and stretch in lines the vegetable wool;
> with teeth of steel its fibre-knots unfurl'd
>   and with the silver tissue clothed the world.

What a good solid name is Arkwright. It conjures visions of northern phlegm and taciturnity, blunt speaking and knowing the value of money. A name which could have come out of any mill or mine. When the founder of this now famous dynasty was born, his parents had no idea that he would revolutionise an industry and die the richest commoner in England and with a title.

This dynasty was firmly rooted in one Richard Arkwright, born the thirteenth child to a Yeoman farmer and tailor of humble circumstances named Thomas and his wife, Ellen, both of Preston, Lancashire in 1732. Of his early life we know nothing, we can only imagine him being inquisitive, playing with engineering and observing how people spun and wove cotton in a county new to such industry, a county in his days that was beautiful with its many small valleys surrounded with moorland, where farmers teased a living growing sheep, cattle, oats and wheat. He would have been familiar with the forces of which water is capable as he watched the water wheels turning to drive the stones that ground the wheat into flour and the effects when, as the snows melted on the moors, the destruction the swollen streams caused to every-thing in their paths. He must have thought early how such forces could be harnessed to benefit the valleys wherein many men who laboured all day operating hand looms, weaving from dawn to dusk and beyond by candle light. Their wives and daughters spent their time spinning by hand to create enough thread to keep the hungry loom alive, to be made faster by the invention of Kay's flying shuttle of 1773.

The balance thus struck was a convenient one. The man at his loom and his womenfolk at their wheels. As the daughters were married off a shortage of thread became a problem. Also at this time the sons were marrying and setting themselves up as weavers in their own right. Many of them treated spinning and weaving as a part time activity when an extra few shillings could be made to supplement their income as farmers. In Lancashire today can be seen farms with an adjoining shop which once housed a loom. This work fitted in well with the weeks when farming was difficult, when the harsh winters driving in from the Irish Sea and the snow from the north made working the land impossible.

Lancashire became an obvious place for the cotton industry to grow, plenty of people versed in hand loom weaving of cotton and fustain, cheap transport costs to take the raw materials from the port of Liverpool and a cheap route for exporting the finished cloth. Later, when Richard had revolutionised cotton manufacture, the many steams would provide the water to power the new spinning machines. Being the watershed of the Pennines created these ample supplies of water which would eventually drive the spinning machinery, but the weavers had to wait for Arkwright and his new machine before this was possible.

His family was industrious – his uncles and cousins were skilled in various trades. Richard had little education, indeed one can assume that an education as available at that time would have stunted his mental growth rather than encourage it. As a consequence his English was poor and his spelling always a problem for him with poor grammar – his later letters bear witness to this. He was, first and foremost a practical man, one of many who created the machines which drove the industrialisation of Britain.

In 1750 Richard was apprenticed to a barber and peruke – or wig – maker, a Mr Pollit, of Bolton. He had already ended a three year apprenticeship with a barber near Preston. He probably took up this profession as he had asthma and found it to be easier on his health than the rigours of moorland farming. He started his apprentice-ship as a lather boy, progressing to shaving then to hair cutting and finally to wig making. Handling hair whilst making wigs would give him a feel for fine thread and an eye for detail., as well as a sense of business for wigs did not come cheap and Richard must have been aware early that money could be made out of fashion, all to come into their own in the near future. He also learned how to run a business for Mr Pollit died whilst Richard was still an apprentice and Richard carried on the business on behalf of the widow until 1755. During this time he became friendly with a Thomas Ridgeway, a master dyer and bleacher of Bolton and through him he met a Robert Holt, a schoolmaster. Both of these men were to form part of Richard's early career in different ways.

Out of this unpromising background was created a man of huge ambition. It is a truism that every great inventor or entrepreneur is driven by some great force. In Richard's case it was a consuming desire to be a man of some importance. He felt his poverty, being the thirteenth son was not a promising situation. There was little to inherit and even less when divided between so many children. He had dealt with the better off whilst making and fitting wigs – his clientele was of "the better sort" – and he must have generated a certain envy of their fine clothes, their carriages and their life style. This burning ambition to not only copy but outclass them drove him until the day he died.

On 31st March, 1755, Richard married Robert Holt's daughter, Patience. He left the widow and started on his own, with a loan from Robert Holt, as a barber-surgeon and wig maker with a secret wig dye of which we know nothing. Thomas Ridgway said of him at this time : "he was always thought clever in his peruke making business and very capital in Bleeding and tooth drawing." Sadly Patience, having given birth to Richard Junior on 19th December, 1755, died leaving Richard Senior a widower with a son to raise. Robert Holt then disowned Artwright for reasons unknown but one wonders if the father did not approve of the marriage in the first place or blamed him for his daughter's death or failed to repay the loan. The animosity was such that Holt excluded any reference to Arkwright or his grandson on his daughter's memorial in Bolton Churchyard. Why had Arkwright not undertaken to provide a memorial for his dead wife?

In March of 1761 he married his second wife, Margaret Biggins of nearby Pennington, and with her dowry of £400 they bought better premises and a beer house – the Black Boy in Bolton. Having spent money on trying to improve these premises he sold up and occupied himself in wig making, a fashion accessory of that time for men. His inventiveness came to the fore when he devised a method of diverting the smoke from his chimney through a clock such that it had every appearance of being a smoke driven time-piece. This would appear to have been a rare demonstration of humour from him.

Others were busy in Lancashire at this time. Men were busy trying to mechanise the spinning of cotton thread. The spinning wheels in common use were each operated by a single woman and whilst they could be very adept at producing large quantities of spun thread, the looms were hungry for more and a speedier method was needed. This was initially satisfied by the spinning jenny which was invented 1764/7. This ingenious machine, still hand operated, could wind sixteen spindles at a time, a major step forward. By 1788 it was said that there were around 20,000 in use of which many would have been in Lancashire. Arkwright must have been aware if not familiar with them. However, the jenny did not provide the whole answer to spinning for the roving had to be prepared by hand beforehand. Roving is the loosely spun rope of fibres which was prepared on the old wheels. Also, the jenny could only produce thread for use as the weft (or woof), the threads that were carried by the shuttle. And as already mentioned, the flying shuttle had already been invented by John Kay, thus speeding up the weaving of cloth.

Arkwright started to experiment with a machine of his own design and here we have a problem for there is a strong case for the previous work of others being used. Defoe stated "When Lewis Paul and Richard Arkwright came forward with their spinning machines, the one in 1738 and the other in 1768, the ground had been prepared for them". This situation occurs with most of the great inventions. Arkwright must have realised the need for a spinning machine which would create thread suitable for both the weft and the warp of a loom. However, now we have Messrs Thomas Highs a Swedenborgian and a John Kay - a different Kay to the flying shuttle one. Highs was a reed maker from Leigh and Kay was a clockmaker from Warrington. A useful pair for they each had skills to add to those of Arkwright. We know little of what they did towards Arkwright's invention but it is likely that one of them had part invented a new type of spinning machine using the mechanical skills of the other to make it. Arkwright took Kay on board and and they proceeded to improve the machine.
They worked long hours in a basement cellar, away from prying eyes, for the area was alive with machinery inventors and entrepreneurs and this new partnership was fearful of copyists. They laboured on a new machine which Arkwright had contri-

buted to, working long hours such that Arkwritht's new wife was so angry that she destroyed their latest machine. This act was to anticipate the later failure of the marriage when at Cromford.

With financial backing from a David Thornley, a merchant of Liverpool and a John Smalley, a publican of Preston, Arkwright and Kay moved to premises in Preston in 1768. They rented a room in the schoolmaster's house near to the parish church, where they worked on their new machine. They spread it about via the schoolmaster that they were working on a new contraption for determining the longitude! This was a device to satisfy inquisitive persons. From this one can deduce that they were working on something which they wanted to protect from plagiarists. The financing was necessary as they were not earning during this period and they had to provide for their own sustenance and shelter as well as seven guineas(£7.35) a year rent for the room.

Their experimenting created strange noises which were likened to "the devil tuning his bagpipes and Arkwright dancing to them". Their patience and endeavour were rewarded for they produced a machine which was to become Arkwright's "throstle", so called as it made a noise similar to a Song Thrush's whistling. It may be aprocryphal but it was said that Arkwright's idea came from watching red hot iron bars being drawn through rollers to make them thinner and in a uniform shape. This is unlikely given that he would have been aware of earlier work undertaken by two men, John Wyatt – a carpenter – and Lewis Paul – the son of a refugee from France, who had used rollers for drawing thread some years before. Their attempt to sell their invention to a mill owner in Birmingham failed.

The breakthrough came when Arkwright and Kay used a system of rollers having different tensions and speeds which would produce even thread which was not too thick or too thin. As with all great inventions the principal sounds simple, but the two inventors must have spent many hours trying and experimenting to get it to perform to their satisfaction. They must have suffered many disappointments which would have caused lesser men to give up. It is to the eternal credit of Artwright and Highs that they overcame all the problems of setting many speeds and distances and the permu-tations of both such that it would work at a reasonable speed without breaking threads and to produce thin but strong thread, thread which could be used for the warp and the weft – or woof. Prior to this, linen and woollen warps were used as cotton was prone to breaking under the strain. Some cotton yarn was imported from India, the rest was spun in Britain by women and girls. From this we get the spinster.

Suddenly, Arkwright along with Kay and Smalley appeared in Nottingham where they occupied a mill on Woolpack Lane in the Lace Market area of Nottingham. They had already witnessed the attacks by frame breakers in Lancashire, some of his machines in a mill at Chorley had been damaged and Hargreave's house had already been burnt to the ground causing him to migrate to Nottingham also. Nottingham was an obvious choice at that time, for it was already established as a centre for the stock-ing industry where skilled frame makers and operators were available as well as a demand for fine cotton thread. This was in 1768, the same year that Arkwright filed his patent for "a new Piece of Machinery never before found out, practised, or used for the Making of Weft of Yarn from Cotton, Flax and Wool". The funding for this came from two kinsmen, John Smalley and David Thornely, but new bankers were needed to allow Arkwright to continue to achieve his ambitions. In the same year and independent of Arkwright, James Hargreaves of Blackburn also came to Nottingham.

His mill on Woolpack Lane was small and he used a horse walking round a gin to drive his machinery. He had some financial backing from an Ichabod Wright, a timber and iron merchant of Nottingham who founded a bank in 1759. It was Samual Need who took over from Wright to partner Arkwright in his venture. The infrastructure in Nottingham suited his purpose. It was a city just starting to boom after the adoption of the stocking frame, which had been invented by the Reverend William Lee in 1589, and the curate in a nearby village called Calverton. Whilst Lee was refused a licence by both Queen Elizabeth I and King James I, he took his invention to France where he died a pauper. His invention was the most complicated machine made up to that time, for it had 3,500 components and took fifty days to make plus twelve for assembly. Later the frame was used by London stockingers and it soon migrated back to the area of its birth, Nottingham. Therefore, Arkwright could tap a source of labour experienced in the use of fine thread with the trade of framesmith forming an important ingredient. He also had already market with stockingers crying out for more and more thread, for stockings had become a favoured fashion accessory for men and women alike. Nottingham was to become one of the triumvirate: Nottingham for cotton hosiery, Leicester for wool and Derby for silk.

One problem would not go away. The frame breakers were getting to be active in the Nottingham area and their spectre started to haunt Arkwright. These people were known as Luddites who had already started on the stocking frames. It is of interest to note that the Luddites and their Majestys' reasons for wanting to ban the stocking frames were the same – they were trying to protect the livelihood of the hand knitters. A legend grew up about the Luddites of Nottingham, for there was a popular belief that they had an intelligent ring leader called King Ludd or Ned Ludd. Some thought this person could have been the infamous Lord Byron whose estate was local and who had much sympathy for those who were denied a living due to these new machines. This rumour came about after Byron – "mad, bad and dangerous to know" – had made an impassioned plea on their behalf in the House of Lords.

Arkwright was also unhappy with horse power. He was ambitious and wanted to have numerous of his inventions to operate which would have required many horses, each of which would take space walking round many gin circles and they would need feeding and all those other additional costs that muscle power required. Arkwright had already considered water power. There was nothing new to this, corn had been ground and bellows to furnaces blown by water power since before the Conqueror's time. Also, Arkwright would have been aware of the water powered mill on the River Derwent in Derby. This mill was undoubtedly the first water powered thread spinning mill in Britain if not in the world. It had started its life in 1704 when a Thomas Cotchett, a barrister of Mickleover, built a silk mill on an island in the river Derwent

– the By-Flatt – where there were three fulling mills. His reasons were the same as Arkwright's, to provide quality thread to supply the weavers. He was also distancing himself from the Guilds of London who determined wage rates and prices. A water wheel of 13.5 feet (4.12m) diameter was installed which rose and fell with the level of the river, which could vary considerably throughout a year. The genius who installed this wheel was another Lancastrian, a George Sorocold of Ashton in Makerfield, who had already constructed a water wheel under the first arch of London Bridge which pumped river water from the Thames to a holding tank and thence to supply part of the capital city.

This powered mill was a sensation and paved the way for future inventors who worked on machinery for the manufacture of cloth, they all owed a huge debt to Cotchett and Sorocold. Their mill was 62 ft (18.9m) long and 35 ft (10.7m) wide and had three storeys. Nothing like it had been seen before. The wheel drove eight spinning machines having a total of 1,340 spindles.

Where one man fails another seems to succeed for sadly Cotchett did fail and a Thomas Lombe of London took the venture over. Lombe with his brother John had been silk merchants and had accrued sufficient capital, a necessity that Cotchett lacked. Tradition has it that John Lombe had been to Leghorn, Italy in 1715 and had spied on their silk machines. Undoubtedly, the Italians had made considerable advances in silk thread production. This sounds credible enough but the aftermath sounds more like a fantasy. John was supposedly pursued to England by the Italians who used a temptress to seduce him, leading to his being poisoned. The stuff of Hollywood rather than Derby! This was followed by Thomas Lombe patenting his machine to spin silk. With Sorocold's help they built a new mill in 1717, retaining Cotchetts mill complete with his machinery. We would be departing from the story of Arkwright if we carry this tale further, sufficient to say that it would be an unreason-able assumption if Arkwright were ignorant of these activities, indeed he most likely visited the mill and had familiarised himself with the details of water powered spin-ning. We cannot imagine today when we take manufacture for granted, with modern mills electrically powered with superb light and adequate heating (or cooling), the impact this silk mill was to have. It would have counted as one of the wonders of the world.

The Nottingham venture ended by being nothing more than initial trial. Arkwright set out to find a site which would suit all his purposes: a "green" labour force, water for power and a consistent supply at that, as far as possible from the Luddites and with connections to the market place. He must have known of Cromford, and many other Derbyshire villages, when he went on horse back as a wig maker buying human hair, a source of some significant income to a poor family. He must have had his sights on many locations which could be suitable for his needs, but finally he chose Cromford.

Cromford at that time was a lead mining, sheep rearing and stocking making community, spread unevenly about the Crume Book and Bonsall Brook, sheltered in a steep fold of the hills, plenty of building stone and timber for building mills and another most tempting asset – whilst the Bonsall Brook could be and still is capricious, the Cromford Sough supplied a generous quantity of water all year round and at a temperature above freezing point.

As when he was experimenting he needed capital, this time he needed a lot of finance to achieve his dream of a factory to house numerous of his new machine, the throstle, with a water wheel to power them. Again he had to turn to backers and he found two: Jedidiah Strutt a silk mill owner of Derby, born at South Normanton and Samuel Need a mercer and later a banker of Nottingham. These were Arkwright's third and fourth backers. Whether this was due to Arkwright having the gift of persuasion or to their understanding of his machine we cannot tell. It could have been a combination of both. Nevertheless the funding became available for work was started on a five storey mill and the water channels needed to drive his wheel. Significantly he did not use the adjacent River Derwent as a power source, he chose the lesser water supplies of the Crume and Sough. There was a mill nearby which used a wheel located in the river to drive the bellows for a lead smelting furnace and a corn mill on the Crume and it was on this latter site that Arkwright built his mill and where the smelter stood he was to build his own church.

On 1st August, 1771, Arkwright and his partner Smalley from his Lancashire days and his two new backers signed a lease for renting the site and the water rights for a payment of £14 per annum. Work started and a house – Steephill (Steeplehouse?) Grange – was bought and demolished, the stone being used for the mill. Steeplehouse, high on the road leading from Wirksworth was, prior to the dissolution of the monasteries, a monastic grange having large barns. It was the ready prepared stone of these large barns which attracted Arkwright, they saved the cost of quarrying and many masons. Spinning had started by March, 1772 in an unsecured building. This is surprising given that Arkwright had become almost paranoid, with reason, that his invention would either be spied upon or broken. During this period he was hiring labour, skilled and unskilled, to help with the building of the machinery and operating it. In 1771 he had advertised in the Derby Mercury for "2 journeymen Clock-Makers, or others that understands Tooth and Pinion well: also a Smith that can forge and file – likewise 2 Wood Turners that have been accustomed to Wheel-making, Spoke-turning, etc." Good rates of pay were being offered for journeyman clock makers, wood turners, filers and smiths. This set a precedent for manufacture throughout the country where these crafts would be used to build complicated machines for working thread and cloth as well as for steam engines. A new profession was created – the millwright. He was clearly making his own machines on the mill site using iron castings of local manufacture, possibly from Hurt's foundary at Alderwasley nearby. Interestingly, a patent had been taken out in 1769 by "Richard Arkwright of Nottingham, clockmaker."

The machinery was driven by an under-shot water wheel, so the water works, if only in part, had been laid out. These latter were very complicated, whereby they collected the water of Bonsall Brook into a mill pond to the rear of the Greyhound Hotel from whence they ran in a channel, combining with the water from the Sough the mouth of which is in the "Bear Pit" behind the shops on Cromford Hill. Initially the water from the Sough was captured in a dam via an underground channel which caused flooding in the mine. A long legal case was fought between Arkwright and the sough proprietors resulting in the latter winning, with Arkwright having to remedy the drainage problem from the sough and having to pay £20 per annum rent for the water. It was later calculated that the quantity of water from these two sources was 5.6 tons (5.7 tonnes) of water from the brook and 71.5 tons (72.6 tonnes) from the sough, per minute. These figures were calculated by the Cromford Canal Company in 1791 and represent a total of nearly 25 million gallons (114 million litres) every 24 hours. And herein lies the weakness of the enterprise of which more later. The supply of water, in spite of the generosity of the brook and sough must have been a worry for there is evidence that Boulton and Watt installed an 8 hp (6 kW) steam engine to pump water from the River Derwent to supply the wheel, a common use for these engines at these times.

The mill was functional and had no architectural merit. It stood six storeys high. Arkwright wanted his mill built quickly and as cheaply as possible. Trimmings would come with his later mill, Masson Mill, but for the time being he wanted to be in production as soon as possible so that his debts could be paid off.

Production was well under way by the end of 1792, producing a thread suitable for calico and cotton, but not suitable as he had hoped for the finer threads for Nottingham lace and the stockingers. Fashion was dictating a need for very fine hosiery and lace, which in turn required a very fine but very strong thread which would withstand the tensions created by the framework knitters' machine and the advent of the lace machine. The best and finest machine lace used Flemish flax, which was as fine as the finest silk, something Arkwright failed to equal. This must have been a disappointment to Arkwright given that one of his reasons for building his mill at Cromford was to capture the Nottingham trade, being only 26 road miles away. It was another invention, not by Arkwright but by Samuel Crompton which made such fine thread possible and that was his spinning mule.

Arkwright's other problem was the tax levied on unprinted calicoes and a ban on printed ones, an unreasonable law intended to protect our famous wool industry. In 1736 this tax had been reduced for fustians (cotton weft, flax warp). The new thread made by Arkwright could do both so it was in his interest and that of his partners, to get the law changed. In 1774 they took their problem to Westminster where they submitted a petition which won approval provided that their thread contained a blue thread or threads and was stamped "British Manufactury". This together with a reduction in tax opened the door for the manufacture and use of Arkwright's thread.

This also opened up the cotton spinning and weaving industry of Lancashire from whence Arkwright came. They already had a tradition of making fustian, a twilled coarse cotton fabric which included such cloth as velveteen, corduroy and so called moleskin beloved of Navvies.

Arkwright's next move, one which was almost as important as his throstle was to patent a carding machine. Hitherto carding was done by hand by scraping two boards of wood having bent metal pins across raw cotton in order to both force the minute threads straight and ready for spinning and to remove unwanted debris. This move was logical, for to rely on hand carding would have needed an army of carders. A patent covering a carding machine along with many other devices, some of which were never pursued, was granted in 1775.

This placed all the processes of thread manufacture in a factory, powered by water. It only left stocking making and finishing industries such as bleaching and dyeing outside his factory. To control the stockingers he built the first industrial village in the world, the Cromford that we know today. In so doing he built good, functional and solid houses having three floors excluding cellars if they had any. The third floor of these terrace houses had a gallery which ran the length of the row, such that one could climb into the top floor in any one house and conceivably climb down into any other of the houses in the row. This idea was to enable the maximum number of stocking frames into the space, to assist in the distribution of cotton thread amongst the weavers and to encourage self help when a loom broke down. The weaving was strictly for the men, fathers and sons. Most were lead miners tempted into a dry and warm working atmosphere, with regular work and regular wages.

The women and children worked in the mill, and the hours were long and at times punishing. There is no record that Arkwright used the iniquitous system of buying parish apprentices for his mills, a system that brought ill repute at another mill in the county, Ellis Needham's at Litton. These mill owners are the ones which gave the profession a bad name by using methods which bordered on physical abuse. Sadly the memory of these employers lingers on and colours our vision, unfairly of those times. Arkwright was not one of these. He did expect a good day's work, for which he paid a fair wage with several benefits thrown in. Of these benefits, apart from the housing, would be in the form of loans advanced for the purchase of a cow and the creation of a market in the village. The Derby Mercury records in 1783 that Arkwright "generously gave 27 of his principal workmen, twenty-seven fine milch cows, worth from £8 to£10 each, for the service of their respect families." Two annual balls were held at the Greyhound Hotel with a week's "jubilee" at the same time. The Honourable John Byng recorded in his diary, "the Landlord (Greyhound Hotel) had under his care a grand assortment of prizes, from Sir Richard Arkwright, to be given at the end to such bakers, butchers and c., as shall have best furnished Sir Richard's prudence and cunning; for without ready provisions, his colony could not prosper." He also sponsored sick clubs and provident societies for medical treatment and sick pay. Every September a "candle lighting" festival was provided when a band escorted the workers to the mill where they were entertained with music and dancing helped along with food and beer. He provided a corn mill for the use of the village with a grain drying kiln, store and miller's cottage, using the Bonsall Brook to drive the wheel.

This benevolence had a price. The workers were tied by living in cottages owned by the employer – lose the job – lose the home. Arkwright demanded and got unswerving loyalty, for example his workers had to sing:

> "Come let us all join in one,
> and thank him for all favours done;
> Let's thank him for all favours still
> Which he hath done beside the mill"

One wonders to which tune this was carolled.

His pay rates were reasonable for the period. In Sir Frederick Eden's "The State of the Poor" of 1797 it is recorded that Arkwright was paying his workers; children of 8 to 14 years – 1 to 5 shillings (10-25p), adult women – 3-5 shillings (15-25p) and overseers – 12 shillings (60p), all per week.

In 1776 the Arkwright partners started a second mill a floor higher than his first at seven storeys. The two 15 ft (4.6m) wheels were over-shot and used the water discharged from the first mill. These wheels were placed in a deep pit in the centre of the mill to reduce the shafting distance between the wheel and the machines. This was in production by September of this year and its opening was celebrated in style. There was a party for the builders where the beer flowed and everyone had a good time. This meant that his employees increased in number considerably and they were coming from as far away as Winster, walking over the uplands which their lead mining ancestors had walked before them. Walking long distances sounds unreason-able to us in the age of the motor car but was not so to the people of those times. They thought nothing of walking several miles to visit a relative on the Sabbath or to work on any other day. He employed an increasing number of children, mostly the off-spring of his female labour force especially the girls, the boys would be learning from their fathers how to tackle and operate a frame at home.

To expand his ownership of land, he bought the estate and manor of Willersley from a Thomas Hallet Hodges. A wise and timely move, for it gave him free reign to build what and where he liked. He was to buy the Manor of Cromford also from Peter Nightingale a lead merchant and smelter of nearby Lea, thus making him the Lord of the Manor. He obtained a charter, dated 1790, to hold a market every Saturday and he built the Greyhound Hotel to overlook the market place. This building was used to provide accommodation for Arkwright's many visitors, as well as providing a focal point and place of congregation for the village.

His first mill was completely lost in a disastrous fire in 1777 and was promptly rebuilt.

A little further up the Derwent valley stood a paper mill in the ownership of Robert Shaw of Snitterton (the 5th Duke of Devonshire's mine agent at the Ecton Copper

Mines, Staffordshire and who later embezzled £1000 and later still £500 for which he was fired and his assets sold off, nonetheless, he went on to buy the paper mill in question) and George White of Winster (who operated lead mines at Llwyn Llwyd in Wales in the 1780s). At this time White was the owner of the Lumb Smelting Mill near Tansley which was water powered from the Bentley Brook. This new mill building was reputed to have been built on an island in the river Derwent. If this be so, there is no trace of it today. An indenture dated from 1783 refers to this new mill being built "at or near a decoy". This lease was for 90 years at an annual rent of £1.00. a further grant of 1772 to George White and John Shore empowered them to carry water to the paper mill from Ball Eye Sough in Bonsall Hollow for a period of 21 years. This was achieved by mining an adit from the sough to a portal to the rear of Cromford Court. The levels suggest that this would be doubtful. A further uncon-firmed report suggests that water was taken from Hagg Mine on the opposite bank of the river, the water being pumped by water wheel. This mill operated until 1811 and appears to have been revived later for there were numerous paper makers in Cromford in the 1840s. In 1811 forty people made brown, blue and white paper using old rope, brown paper, coarse cotton and white rags. The paper during manufacture was pressed, separated and dried, taking two men to make ten reams (5,000 sheets) per day. When part of Masson Mill was demolished in 1955, the foundations of the paper mill were revealed.

Arkwright bought his partners out and built a mill of brick having six storeys, the bricks being produced locally at Alderwasley and Steeple Hill. This new mill was named Masson Mill after the adjoining and dominant hill, using water power from the River Derwent. This mill was embellished as can be seen today, with so called Venetian windows and a neat louvred cupola intended for a bell and sporting a weather vane. He placed a weir across the river built down-curved and not up-curved as was customary. The wheels at this mill were replaced in 1922 and are still in situ and are capable of operating turbines if required to drive electricity generators. The mill was much added to in later years.

Masson Mill employed many children, who worked 13 hours a day with a 40 minute break for dinner. They lodged in a large house near to the mill, now gone. The boys were paid 3s.6d. (17.5p) per week and the girls 2s.3d. (11.1p) per week. They were required to attend the local chapel and its Sunday School, the same that was to become the Lady Glenorchy Chapel. A commentator of the time recorded, "one of Arkwright's most original achievements was discipline in his Mills, he made his presence felt but did not overwork his employees, they *only did 12 hours by a day shift and 12 hours by a night shift*, when other firms usually worked 14 hour shifts. We do not have the employees view of this utopia! (The italics are the author's.)

Using the Derwent was a bold move on Arkwright's part, brought about by a desire to carry on building mills with his original site filling, for the space left here was destined for warehousing. Arkwright had a fear of this fast flowing and turbulent river, for he had witnessed the destruction it could cause when in flood. On the completion of his new Masson Mill, Arkwright had finished with his factory building at Cromford. He added warehouses at his original site to complete his mill complex by 1791. Significantly, the warehouse at the roadside has no windows on the ground floor elevation, his fear of frame breakers or spies?

What an achievement this was! From a wig maker in Lancashire living off borrowed money to a millionaire – in the coin of his time – in 23 years. He now had his carriage and his fine house – Rock House – which still overlooks his mill complex at Cromford. He bought his partners out, Need had already died of old age. Smalley retired to Wales after many arguments with the mill manager when Strutt acted as an arbitrator and Strutt himself was paid off. Strutt had plenty to do with his new fact-ories at Belper and Milford, where his invention, the "Derby Rib" machine was busy making hosiery; gloves and mittens coming later. Before being paid off Arkwright and Strutt bought Smalley's share inherited by his son for £10,750 (£11 million in today's coin). Thornley had died in 1772 at the early age of 31 years. His widow Marjorie, said that Arkwright "had frightened him off."

Arkwright was on his own now and he prospered. His patents were licences to make money and make money he did, such that he gave each one of his ten children a Christmas present of £10,000.

Suddenly, in 1785, when Arwright had achieved his dream and was settling back to enjoy his gains, two names from his past appeared to plague him, his old partners Thomas Highs and John Kay who issued a writ of *scire facias* (requires a person to appear and show why a record should not be enforced or annulled) against Arkwright. The Lancashire mill owners were seeking to have Arkwright's patents disallowed on the grounds that he was not the inventor. This is an oft repeated feature with the advances in technology of that time and obviously born of jealousy of Arkwright's riches and life style. However, in hindsight we might allow some sympathy for Highs and Kay, for they had helped Arkwright in his early days, contributing their time, money and expertise in the days when they worked hard and long hours perfecting the new inven-tion. In a sense Arkwright brought this upon himself for making a fuss about the infringement of his patent. The questions that had to be addressed by the jury were three in number: 1) is the invention new? 2) is it invented by the defendant?; 3) was it sufficiently described in the specification?

They won, in spite of a sixteen year silence, and the letters patent were cancelled by the jury after the hearing. Arkwright was undoubtedly angry but he had little to worry about, for he had already made his fortune and he was still in business supplying hungry outlets. He threatened to make them pay, more easily said than done. He had to be satisfied with his dubbing them the "Lancashire rascals" who were breaching his patent anyway! He vowed revenge, a vow more easily uttered than acted on, it appears that nothing came of his threat.

In 1785, Arkwright undertook the rationalisation of the water courses which still ran on the surface open to the sky. They were undoubtedly becoming a nuisance to people and traffic, so he decided to divert them underground by the "cut and shut" method. In the same year, along with the new water system, he changed the under-shot wheel of his mill for a new over-shot one, a more efficient use of water when the head available is low. The sough was cut back from its portal in the Market Place to the Bear Pit. Water from the Pit did however have a tunnel to the mill pond to relieve excessive flow.

He still hung on to his Nottingham mill, which was converted to steam power by the famous Boulton and Watt partnership in 1790, ten years after the one they had installed at Cromford.

He had a considerable bonus when he was knighted in 1786 to become Sir Richard Arkwright, not for his industry or his inventions but for services to the community following a speech of loyalty delivered on behalf of the Wapentake of Wirksworth on the failure of an assassination attempt on King George III. His mansion, his "castle" was under construction in an enviable location only minutes from his mills, he had built mills or licensed his inventions to mills along the Derwent valley and its tributaries and further afield. It was said that he made £700 for every 100 spindles installed and had investments worth £200,000.

By 1788 his patent had been used to build 143 factories and he was a shareholder in 110, distributed as follows:

Derbyshire	22
Nottinghamshire	17
Lancashire	41
Wales	17
Scotland	13

with an interest in twenty mills in the Derwent valley alone.

So the reputation of Arkwright was known for many miles around, at a time when communication was by horse drawn stages on poor roads. However, it was not all easy going. Arkwright proved how ruthless he could be, by ignoring the interests of the Dukes of Rutland and Devonshire when damming and diverting the steams in their ownership. The Duke of Rutland sued Arkwright for trespass and won, leaving Arkwright to pay compensation and £10 per annum for the right to use the water. Such costs were minimal given his weath, it was therefore a hollow victory for the Duke.

Titus Salt of Bradford sought Arkwright's help when he built his own industrial village, Saltaire complete with workers' housing, a church, a cotton mill but no public house or beer house. His mills and housing were wondered at from beyond our shores, for a mill was built at Ratingen, Germany by 1783 and was named Cromford, being the first water powered cotton mill on mainland Europe. See Appendix VI.

He was also the progenitor of the Cromford Canal (Act of Parliament, 1789), referred to elsewhere.

In 1787 he was made High Sheriff of the County of Derby. He could now look back on his life with much satisfaction for he had achieved not only the social status that he longed for; a knighthood, High Sheriff, Lord of his own Manor, self made millionaire, a scion of the local gentry and the largest industrialist in the country if not in the world, but he could also look at the many mills which he had built or financed.

Alas, he did not live long enough to occupy his Willersley Castle, for it burned down one night after a careless workman had left a lantern burning near to combustible materials. Sir Richard Arkwright Kt died in 1792, a millionaire several times over and it was said that he was the richest commoner in England. This comment says much about where the wealth lay in England at that time and that we had produced our first self made millionaire, a trend which had thus started would grow over the ensuing years. He was buried in the churchyard at St Gil4es, Matlock Town to be disinterred and reburied in his own crypt in his own chapel, St Mary's, built at his cost.

So what do know about this man? His portrait by Joseph Wright of Derby shows a man having a pot belly and jowls, a man accustomed to a good table, also a man at peace with himself. Unfortunately for him, he suffered from asthma, which is a grie-vous affliction today, how much worse it must have been 200 years ago. His eyes, the windows of the soul, suggest a man who knows what he is about and how to do it, a man who will breach no argument. He distanced himself from his children and in later life he became lonely. There was talk of his having a "lady" of Bakewell who visited him regularly at Rock House for his personal comforts.

As to his character, we have conflicting reports, some must be honest, but some may be from the pens of malicious people who may have had an axe to grind or were just jealous of him and his achievement.

Given below is a selection of some of the written comments about his character, with their sources.

7th August, 1781
Matthew Boulton to his partner James Watt

"It is agreed by all who know him that he is a Tyrant and more absolute than a Bashaw … if he had been a man of sense and reason he would not have lost his patent"

A "bashaw" is a haughty man – from the Turkish "pasha".

One can only wonder at this, for surely he had to be a man of supreme sense and reason to have achieved the many things he had. This comment was made at about the time that Arkwright was looking into the use of a steam engine in his factory in Nottingham.

Sir Robert Peel
Minutes of Evidence taken before the Select Committee of the Children employed in the Manufactories of the United Kingdom, 1816

" ... a man who has done more honour to the country than any man I know, not excepting our great military characters."

William Nicholson
A "superior genius" and "cunning schemer and collector of other mens' inventions, supporting them by borrowed capital and never afterwards feeling or showing any emotion of gratitude to the one or the other."

Thomas Carlisle
1843 (51 years after his death)

"O reader, what a historical phenomenon is that bag-checked, pot-bellied, Lancashire man, much inventing barber ...... and it was this man that had to give England the power of cotton."

Sylas Neville
The Diary of Sylas Neville, 1767-88

" .... by his conduct appears to be a man of great understanding and to know the way of making his people do their best. He not only distributes pecuniary rewards, but gives distinguishing dresses to the most deserving of both sexes, which excites great emulation. He also gives two balls at the Greyhound (Hotel) to the workmen and their wives and families with a two weeks jubilee at the time of each ball. This makes them industrious and sober all the rest of the year."

Of his mills:
Uvedale Price
Essays on the Picturesque, 1810

"When I consider the striking natural beauty of such a river as that at Matlock, and the effect of the seven storey buildings that have been raised there, and on other beautiful streams, for cotton manufactories, I am included to think that nothing can equal them for the purposes of disbeautifying an enchanting piece of Scenery; and that economy had produced, what the greatest ingenuity, if a prize were given for ugliness, could not surpass."

One can only have some sympathy for this view!

Honourable John Byng
The Torrington Diaries, 1790

"These cotton mills, seven stories high, and fill'd with inhabitants, remind me of a first rate man of war; and when they are lighted up, on a dark night, look most luminously beautiful."

There is a painting by Joseph Wright of Derby which captures this scene.

The motto on his arms:

Multa Tuli Faceque – I have endured much, but I have accomplished a great deal.

ARKWRIGHT OF WILLERSLEY
CO DERBY.

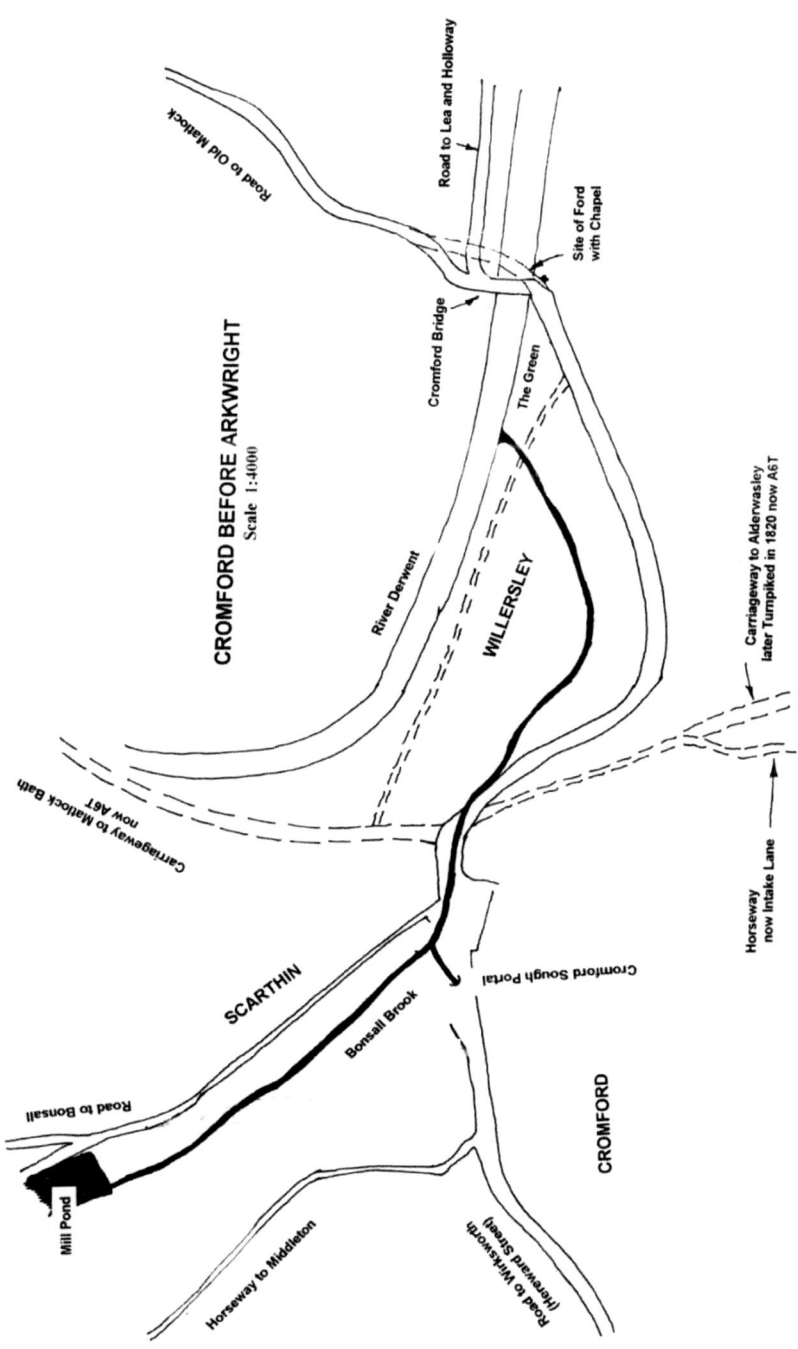

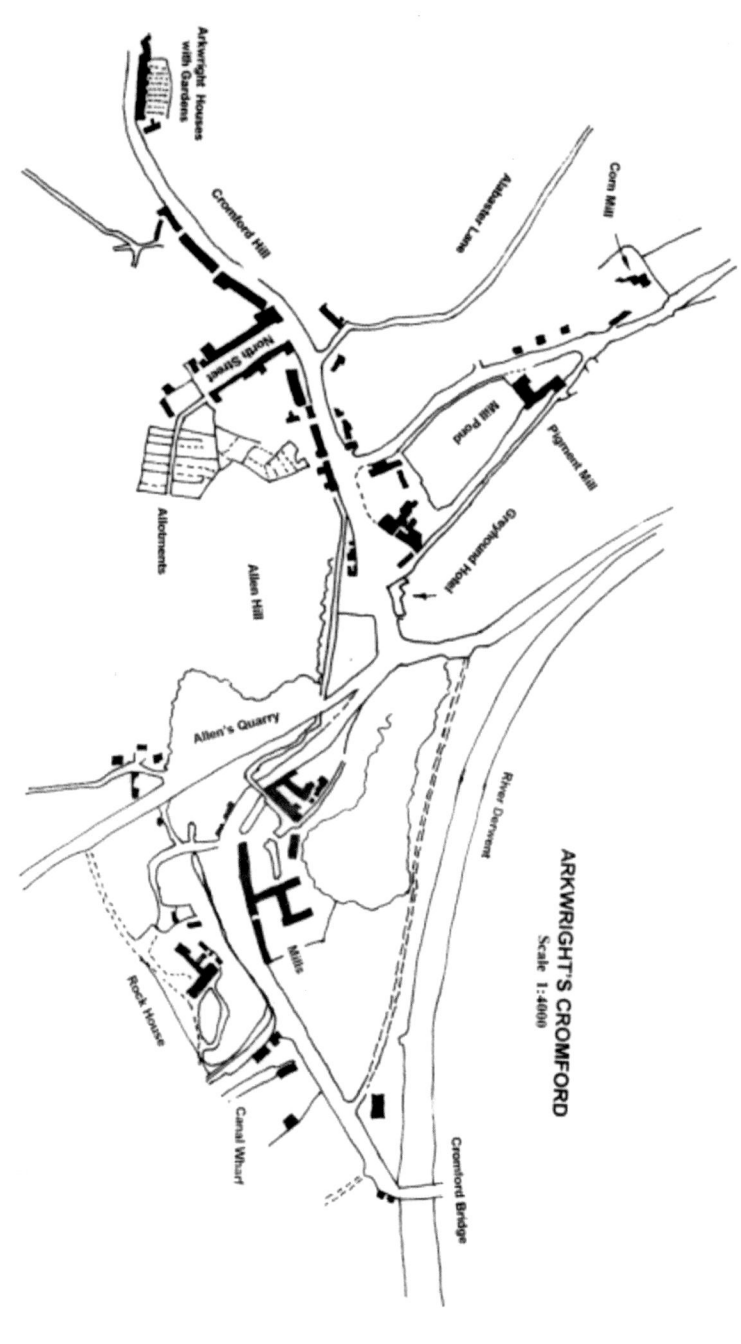

Chapter Five
Arkwright's Legacy

On the death of Arkwright, his spirit was to decline such that his mills went out of family ownership. His inheritor, Richard Jnr, kept the mills for a while but disposed of most of them, for he pursued a different career to that of his father.

Richard Jnr. did not enjoy a close relationship with Sir Richard. He was sent to public school and university, and only the best would do. In spite of Sir Richard's lack of interest in his only son, he was determined that he would be given the education and learn the social graces which were denied him in his impoverished youth in Lancashire.

The empire which Richard Jnr was to inherit was a large one, the first such conglomerate of factories under one name that the world had ever seen. It is easy with hindsight for us to shrug our shoulders at this achievement, we are accustomed to self made men who make millionaires in their own lifetime and to industrial conglomerates. Today these latter are usually the result of take-overs and amalgamations. Arkwright's achievement was to build his empire from scratch and without a precedent. Also, in these days of legislation which covers the workers in their workplace, it is easy for us to criticise these pioneers for working people for long hours and in dangerous situations. They new no better - we must give credit to Arkwright who whilst he was a "hard nosed" business man, he was also a good employer who expected a good day's work for a fair day's pay. His generosity in other matters has been touched upon.

Richard Jnr was to continue these traditions of fatherly benevolence towards not only the workers but also to the village. He does not appear to have the same forcefulness which characterised his father, none of the bluster, non of the total dedication which separated him from his wife and children and which also drew the opprobrium of so many of his contemporaries.

Arkwright's wife had left him in the 1780s and had settled at the Gate House, Wirksworth with her daughter Susannah who was by then Mrs Charles Hurt and where she died in 1835. Here she led a contented existence amongst the people of what was then the second largest town in the county. She played the part of the Lady of the Manor, whilst her husband carried on his life without her and without any need for her.

Richard Jnr was to make another fortune of his own as a banker, a new breed of men at that time. The money which he inherited he lent out at what was considered to be high rates of interest, which we would be happy to pay today. It is said that he doubled his father's capital in his own lifetime.

It must have brought him some smug satisfaction to be lending money to the local aristocracy, the very people who had frowned on Arkwright's lowly birth and were arguably jealous of his financial success. One such aristocrat was Georgiana, Duchess of Devonshire who got herself into financial difficulties - not difficult for such a capricious person - which one assumes were kept from the Duke, for he could easily have repaid any of her debts many times over. One can only gather from this that she wished the matter to be kept secret and she clearly trusted Richard Jnr. In turn, Richard Jnr must have trusted that she would repay, although he had the final sanction - the knowledge of a debt which the Duke would not have wished the Duchess to have incurred without his knowledge.

The correspondence between Richard Jnr and the local swells is considerable and it all reads like any banker's dealings would read. He no doubt took considerable risks for he seemed to operate without collateral, as did many a banker at that time. Today's bankers would blanch with horror at the loans made by Richard Jnr and the lack of security. Perhaps this spirit was what was needed during these burgeoning times and one of the reasons why we became the factory of the world.

By 1792, the Arkwrights were entrenching with their cotton interests, mostly following the death of the founder on 3rd August, 1792. They stuck to the throstle as a means of spinning cotton, but the spinning mule, invented by Samuel Crompton, was gaining in popularity and it was becoming the standard method for spinning. Whilst this was an expensive machine to build, it could wind a large number of bobbins and up to three and sometimes four machines could be handled by one operative. It also produced fine threads which were strong, and like the throstle, suitable for the weft as well as the warp.

The geographical position of Cromford, in spite of the advent of the canal, was becoming a barrier to trade. The sudden growth of the cotton spinning industry in the north-west, especially in Lancashire, Arkwright's place of birth and his early experiments, was robbing mills built in remote valleys like the Derwent. The raw cotton came into Liverpool from whence it was delivered by canal or road to the mills, the finished goods went out the same way. Cromford is a long way from Liverpool or any other port. The route taken by the Romans to the Humber Estuary, via the Rivers Derwent and Trent could have been canalised, indeed the Trent was canalised to the coast early, but this would have taken the goods to a port on the east coast of England. It is a long way round to Britain to despatch boats to the new empire and the United States. Liverpool was so much easier, cheaper and quicker.

The area also started to boom from the proliferation of hydropathic establishments, started by John Smedley of Lea Mills and copied by many others who took advantage of the springs which abound on the hills overlooking the river Derwent. The later advent of the railway only worsened the situation for cotton spinning in the area, for railways also moved the goods in and out of Liverpool with more speed and less expense. The 1860s were a particularly hard time, as the American Civil War raged, Cromford was starved of cotton, Lancashire was taking it all, for they could afford higher prices with low transport costs to find. However, there were sufficient stocks of cotton in the warehouse at Cromford at one stage to supply some mills in Lancashire. This was exceptional for workers were laid off in the 1860s and the villagers suffered from poverty.

Meanwhile Richard Jnr was busy with the village and the estate. He lived in Willersley Castle, something his father never did. He was to enjoy the rewards of his father's hard work in many ways. He was the squire of the parish, the leading citizen and to his credit, his influence was for the good. He rectified the depredations of the miners who had reduced the Cromford end of the Duffield Frith by taking timber for shoring and stempling their mines and for smelting their lead. This they had, and still have a right to, under the then traditions of the field, later ratified with modifications by the Mineral Courts Acts of 1851 and 1852. His solution was to plant 50,000 trees a year for seven years, a total of 350,000 trees, mostly deciduous. These are the trees that we see today which form such an important feature of the countryside about the village, the Via Gellia being such a sound example. In so doing he set the clock back to the time of Domesday, for the plantations in the area exceed the average for woodland which has been calculated as being 26% of the land area of Derbyshire in 1068.

The planting on the hillsides which surround Willersley and the village are landscaped to a set pattern, a landscape which is contrived, there is nothing natural about it. This coupled with the trees planted by the Hurt family further down the valley - Shining Cliff Woods and beyond - make this section of valley so arborious. Whilst one can accept that they were also planted as a crop, they were also planted to provide pleasing vistas. They were for the benefit of the family dynasty for they would not have matured in Richard Jnr's life span. Due to bad management, these same woods are filled with saplings, dead trees and that Derbyshire weed, the sycamore.

Richard Jnr was the only child of Sir Richard's first marriage to Patience Holt who died in 1756, a few months after Richard Jnr was born. One can speculate that one event precipitated the other. Richard Jnr was to marry a local girl from Bonsall, Mary daughter of Adam Simpson, of whom we know little. They were to have eleven children, six male and five female. Alas, two of them, both female, did not make old bones: Mary died in 1803 aged 15 years and Harriet in 1815 aged 17 years. Of Sir Richard's family by his second wife, three girls, one became a spinster and lived with her mother at Wirksworth, two died in infancy.

Of the other of Richard Jnr's girls, two made "good" marriages. This would have pleased Sir Richard's predilection towards the landed classes; Elizabeth married Francis Edward Hurt of Alderwasley, the adjoining estate owner and the other, Anne married Sir James Wigram Bt of Walthamstow who was to distinguish himself as a King's Council, a Member of Parliament and as a Judge. His sister Anne was to marry the Reverend Joseph Arkwright and his brother the Right Reverend Joseph Cotton Wigram, Bishop of Rochester, was to marry Susan Maria Arkwright, daughter of Peter Arkwright (son of Richard Jnr).

Of Richard Jnr's sons, all did well and made good marriages: Richard III of Normanton Turville, Leicestershire and Sutton Scarsdale Hall, Derbyshire married Martha Maria daughter of Reverend William Beresford of Ashbourne, Derbyshire, rector of Sunning in Berkshire, Robert of Stoke Hall, Bakewell and later of Sutton Scarsdale married Frances daughter of Stephen Kemble of Newcastle on Tyne, Peter who was to become the Sheriff of Derbyshire in 1855 married Mary Ann daughter of Charles Hurt of Wirksworth, John who married Sarah the daughter of Sir H Hoskins Bt of Harewood, Herefordshire, Charles who married into the famous Sitwell family, Mary the fifth Daughter of E S W Sitwell of Stainsby Hall, near Smalley, Derbyshire.

For the descendants of the Arkwrights who left the north to settle on estates in the south, the reader is commended to read Hazel Lake's excellent book "The Arkwrights and Harlow", available from the shop at Arkwright's Mill, Cromford for less than £5.00.

The reader is also referred to the pedigree in Appendix II of this book, for the descendants and siblings of the various Cromford Arkwrights. But one other is worthy of special mention: Augustus Peter Arkwright, son of Peter and grandson of Richard Jnr was to become a Commander in the Royal Navy and the Member of Parliament for North Derbyshire, 1868-80. He was also instrumental in helping to found the local Lodge of Free and Accepted Masons. This lodge was consecrated on 24th April, 1874 and was named the Arkwright Lodge taking the Arkwright coat of arms for masonic use. This event was held at the "Terrace Hotel" later to be known as the New Bath Hotel, where the Lodge still meets. It is characteristic of the Arkwright family, that the lodge furniture was bought and gifted by Peter Arkwright (at that time a captain in the Royal Navy) for which generous act he was made a life member. Whilst this lodge was the daughter lodge to another local lodge, it is of interest to note the Lancashire influence, for the bye-laws and ritual were borrowed from a lodge in Manchester. A tradition which was already 89 years old in the county, founding a new lodge to help perpetuate the ideals of this ancient movement.

Also, in the context of Peter Arkwright the father of the above Augustus Peter Arkwright and being the grandson of Sir Richard, the latter would not have been so pleased if he had known that the grandson of his old friend and partner Jedediah Strutt was made Baron Belper. All Peter could muster was to become the Sheriff of the county. This is a measure of how the family had diversified and in some sense declined in prestige over the years.

So what of Richard Jnr's life? Apart from becoming a successful banker, he was an excellent patron to the village. He opened the church for worship by the rest of the village allowing them to use his private carriageway to access it, the same route also being opened to them on Tuesdays and Thursdays. There is some confusion over this, some people believing that the grounds of Willersley castle itself was opened on these two days also, there is no evidence of this.

Richard Jnr ran Masson Mill, where the river still provided enough water power, the mills at Cromford being halted by a lack of water. He admitted to a committee of 1816, which was investigating into the conditions of children working in mills, that 37% of his labour was under eighteen years of age (Strutt at the same time employed 48%) and the company had from 1774 employed children as young as seven years of age. In 1816, he operated a night shift of 164 boys who received extra pay. Several observers noted that these boys were "extremely dissipated" and had only a "few hours sleep". This was not uncommon in mills at that time. Masson Mill had a lodging for these boys formed by joining two or three houses together. It was probably the behaviour of some of these boys which caused Lady Glenorchy to create a chapel here. Masson Mill has been superbly converted into a shopping "Village" and museum. The main entrance sports a fine statue of Sir Richard Arkwright.

When the Upper Mill closed in 1846 and the Lower Mill was burned out in 1890, followed by Frederic Arkwright's selling Masson Mill in 1898, the final Arkwright connections with milling ceased. From then on they farmed the estate, farmed in a loose fashion as land owners who rented to farmers and quarry owners, let shooting rights and enjoyed other income from investments in the canal, railway and other enterprises. The mills in which Sir Richard had had an interest also failed for a variety of reasons: lack of capital, fire - the scourge of all mill owners at that time - selling out and conversion to other uses. The following list, by no means complete, but covering Derbyshire activities, gives some idea of the fate of the original Arkwright empire:

- Calver Mill - operated by John Gardom and John Pares were paying Sir Richard in their hey-day of 1778, £7,000 per annum for the use of patents and £1000 per annum royalty. This mill burned down in 1802 but was rebuilt in the ensuing two years. The 7th Duke of Devonshire bought it in 1860 when it operated 12,000 spindles. This six storeyed monolithic structure which has no architectural merit became the factory for Sissons who manufacture stainless steel holloware and was used for the filming of the television series "Colditz". The two breast shot water wheels of 1827 and 1852 worked until 1955. This mill has now been converted into luxury apartments.

- Bakewell Mill - of 1777 was also burned down in 1868 employed 300-400 women and children. From 1789 it was run by Richard Jnr and from 1829 by Robert and Peter Arkwright.

- Cressbrook Mill - of 1779 and behind the large building of 1815, burned down in 1785 when Richard Jnr sold the land.

- Ashbourne Mill - was operated by J D Cooper, son-in-law of Strutt, replaced in 1865 and demolished in 1996 to make way for a Sainsbury's supermarket.

- Haarlem Mill, Wirksworth - built 1780 but sub-let by Richard Jnr to Madeley, Hacket and Riley later in 1879 to Wheatcrofts for the manufacture of red tape. This is the same red tape used by governments, lawyers and local authorities most of which was manufactured in Wirksworth with some in Derby.

- Marple Bridge, Glossop - built as a warehouse by Sir Richard as a warehouse 1794-1800 to be close to the Peak Forest Canal.

- Mellor (now in Cheshire due to a boundary change) built 1790-91 and operated by Samuel Oldknow with Sir Richard's finance, Richard Jnr taking it over in 1828 on the death of Oldknow. Burned down in 1892.

- Darley Abbey near Derby - built under licence for Thomas Evans in 1771 a very early customer of Sir Richard. Evans also built a model village at Darley Abbey based on Arkwright's principals.

It was Richard Jnr. who built the school, still in use at the end of North Street, the boys school being opened in 1832 and the girls in 1840, having 160 boy and 80 girl scholars in 1846 the head teacher being a Mr William Shaw. The head teacher's salary and other running costs were partly funded by the Arkwrights, the pupils contributing their weekly pennies. These school buildings still provide for the education of today's Cromford children, the premises being only a little altered. The site includes a head teacher's house. The author's cousin Ken Smith was the head teacher within recent memory.

This same school was also used by the community in general. In the 1840s Cromford Philharmonic Society comprising fifty voices and instruments held concerts in the school every three months. One assumed that they practised at the school.

Of the mills at Cromford, the years following the death of the founder were not good. The Upper Mill ceased spinning in 1846 when it was converted into a brewery by William Melville and Company. It lost its two top floors in 1891 to a fire. It was later to become a laundry, in 1921 a colour works - Cromford Colour Company, later Burrell Colours, for a brief spell in the 1970s a Trout Hatchery and finally to be acquired by the Arkwright Society in 1979. It also suffered from a second fire in 1930.

The Lower Mill was still operated by Arkwright and Company as a hosiery warehouse until this was gutted by fire in November, 1890.

Masson Mill remained with Arkwright and Company until 1898 when it was sold to the English Sewing Cotton Company who installed a turbine in the 1920s to take advantage of the available water to provide electricity. This was put into use during the power workers' strike in 1972 and enough electricity was generated to keep some people in work.

The death knell was sounded in 1837 when a new sough to unwater the lead mines in the Wirksworth basin, the Meerbrook Sough, opened its sluice gates. It connected to the Cromford Sough and as it was at a lower horizon, the Cromford Sough was deprived of most of its flow. The wheels could not depend entirely on the Bonsall Brook so they stopped turning. Arkwright's reliance on these water sources was proved to be ill founded, for the only mill which continued working was that which relied on the river which he wished to avoid, the Derwent.

This sough, dealt with in Chapter Three, caused the demise of the cotton milling enterprises of the Arkwrights in Cromford. A legal battle ensued when the Arkwrights challenged the Meerbrook Sough Company on the grounds that they had robbed the mills of an ancient right to water. They lost the case and the sough continued to flow whilst the mill wheels ground to a halt. The mines enjoyed a brief prosperity, the spinning days were over for Cromford.

The Arkwright family scattered, some because of marriage others because of changes in direction. This history of Cromford does not cover them outside the parish, sufficient to say that many made their own way in the world, others lived off the financial legacies of Sir Richard and son.

The Market Place c. 1905
Lloyds Bank was just off this picutre to the left. Note the market shambles as originally intended with Bodens the Boot Maker nex tot the Pharmacy. The ladies with the carriage and groom suggest someone of importance locally, Arkwrights?

Chapter Six
Transport

References in this chapter to the Street implies Hereward Street, the Roman road from Rocester to Chesterfield.

Highways

Early transport in and around Cromford must have been a nightmare until modern times – some might argue that it still is? The valley bottoms of both the River Derwent and Bonsall Brook were prone to flooding in winter with access only possible part way up the hill sides. The same hillsides which would have been heavily wooded, not the trees we see today, and would have been the haunt of wild animals and footpads.

The earliest highway that we know of is the Roman road known to us as Hereward Street, laid by 79-80 AD. Whilst this is disputed by some it is reasonable to assume that the road from Rocester to Chesterfield came through the village and is represented today by Cromford Hill. The Romans would have crossed the Derwent at a ford a little downstream from where the present day Cromford Bridge now stands. The bridge chapel of at least the 15th century has its origins in a ford chapel where the travellers would offer a prayer and light a candle or oil lamp placed in the wall niche or squint for their safe crossing. An inscription made in a stone in the bridge wall "THE LEAP OF MR B H MARE 1697" purportedly refers to a time when a Benjamin Heywood of Bridge House was riding his mare over the bridge when it leapt over the parapet and into the river, both escaping unhurt. There is another version of this story, the one quoted seems likely, except that genealogical research shows a Bernard Heywood had a son Benjamin who died at less than a week old in 1696. This inscribed stone is not in its original location, it having been relocated when the bridge was repaired. The river, before its many alterations, was capricious and was feared by travellers. It certainly frightened Arkwright to such a degree that he refused to use it to drive his mill wheels. He later relented with his Masson mill, he could recall the damage caused to one of the Nightingale's mills by the river when in flood.

Hereward Street would then have climbed up the hill along the route of today's Willersley Lane and the road to Starkholmes. The Romans noted for their straight roads had to make concessions to bends for climbing such steep hills. The Street would have been used for moving men and materials across country and on to Rome. It is known that Derbyshire lead found its way to Italy at this time and would have been carried on the banks of pack horses for export through the Humber estuary. Roman pigs of lead of Derbyshire origin have been found at South Cave near Brough (Petvaria).

This is certainly an ancient highway and like most Roman roads, it already existed in Celtic times – the late Iron Age. The valley therefore was somewhat isolated, but the

Romans were glad to have access in pursuit of their precious lead. The movement of corn, wool and mutton was important to them to provide for local garrisons, the nearest of any importance being Little Chester (Derventio) with baths at Buxton (Aqua Arnametiae).

The movement of lead from Roman times onward was important for Cromford sits in the centre of an area rich in this metal. The nearness of Wirksworth, the administrative centre of mining in the King's Field must have had considerable importance to the village. The lead was traditionally moved in cast pigs slung on the backs of pack animals, usually a pony, with two pigs slung one on each side of the animal. Some of the local footpaths were miners' ways, the pony drivers being known as Jaggers. In the 17th century they were paid one shilling (5p) per day.

These were developed into long trains of pack animals sometimes up to a hundred ponies long. These carried foodstuffs, wool, lead and salt, the ever important preservative of food from the wich's of Cheshire – Northwich, Nantwich, etc. One such pack way climbs from Bonsall Dale to Bonsall Village and beyond. This way climbs up hill from Chapel Lane and used to go by a Hermitage known as Rugg's Hall now quarried away. It also went by the Bloody Stone, the supposed scene of a brutal murder many years ago, no trace could be found of this by the author.

The Derwent valley north of Cromford was only accessible on foot or animal at these times and up to Arkwright's time. The equivalent today would be Lathkill Dale west from Over Haddon. Their route to Matlock, the nearest town other than Wirksworth would have been over the hill to Starkholmes by following the Roman road. The route south was along Intake Lane towards Belper and on to Derby. These track ways were ill maintained and were hazardous, not just from footpads but from subsidence and rock falls. Similarly the way along the Via Gellia would have been nothing better than a pack horse way for miners and smelters.

However the crossing of the Derwent must have been of some importance for a pack horse bridge was built in the 15th century. The original bridge had spans of four metres and was clearly intended to carry wagons as well as ponies. It had pointed arches and side refuges. This connected the pack horse routes from Belper via Wirksworth on the west and with Matlock and Lea and Holloway on the east side. So important was this crossing that it had a bridge chapel of the same date if not earlier. This was in the time of Henry VIII and the bridge was mentioned by Leland and in the will of a Richard Smyth of 1504 which refers to the bridge. When it was widened to its present width, rounded arches were attached to the north or upstream side of the existing structure.

All this changed with the advent of the turnpikes. This system which allowed trusts to be formed for the upkeep of the highways in return for which tolls could be collected was a mixed blessing. Travellers resented having to pay tolls for the dubious benefit of travelling along the King's highway, having enjoyed the privilege for nothing since time immemorial. Many of these trusts undertook their duties conscientiously by maintaining the roads well and keeping them in good order, others took the tolls and ignored the roads.

Hereward Street through Cromford became part of the important turnpike from Birmingham via Derby and to Chesterfield finishing at Sheffield. This following the same route through the village stopping at the Greyhound Hotel where refreshment was available to both the travellers and the horses, before tackling either Cromford Hill to the west or the road to Starkholmes to the east. One can only imagine what the horses had to suffer having to scale these hills in either direction with a coach and passengers in tow. It is likely that as was the custom, the passengers might have had to walk behind the coach up the steep parts with a cock horse connected to help the horses. The names of these coaches conjure up romantic visions: The Times – which came to Cromford via Wirksworth, the Lord Nelson, Lady Nelson, Royal Bruce, Defiance, Peveril of the Peak and the Peak Guide all of which took the valley route from Derby via Belper. All had Manchester as their destination from Birmingham and vice versa.

Eventually a horse way was built to replace the hazardous path of the 1660s in 1702 through the old village of Willersley and at the foot of the rock facing the Willersley Castle. Arkwright did not want an old route as well as the hamlet of Willersley to be in front of the rock to spoil the out look from his new mansion. He therefore diverted the road and destroyed the village. The original highway became his private carriageway in 1795 thus closing the road to St. Mary's church. A footpath can still be walked which traces the route of this road. It was intended as a dramatic access to his mansion, the cast iron (not wrought iron) gates at the A6 end testify to this along with the ruins of a gate house. The occupant of this minuscule dwelling of two rooms was required to control access and ensure that ordinary people did not use it except on Sundays when attending church. It was from this gate that George Eliot – who knew the area well – referred to the view as "the turn of the road at Cromford being esteemed by painters". To divert the road, Arkwright had the cutting made known as Scarthin Nick. It was originally narrower than it is now, it was widened twice, the latest in 1960 to cope with the increase in modern day traffic.

The road from Belper to Matlock via Cromford, now a trunk road the A6T, was a boon for the visitor then as it is now. Nothing changes for J B Frith in 1905 gave this warning: "avoid it on a Summer Saturday or Sunday for then every speck of dust on the road is set dancing by multitudes of traps and cycles and motors and you that have come to bless will stay to curse". Things have not changed, one wonders what he would think of this same scene today?

On the contrary to this, Pilkington eulogised this part of the valley in 1789 as "the most compleat (sic) piece of scenery in the whole valley." It is hard to contradict him even now, over two hundred years later.

The private carriageway was built by Messrs Strutt and Pennel in 1745. This partnership from Nottingham had bought the "thermal" springs at Matlock Bath for a George Wragg for £1000 and were about to exploit them. The royal Hotel, the site now occupied by a car park off Temple Road, was the result of their labours, the attraction being the thermal springs – by definition these are not true thermal springs. Finally, this road was extended to Matlock in 1771. It was on this highway that Lady Glenorchy came to grief. There was a toll bar close to Masson Mill to cover the road to Matlock.

An Act of Parliament of 1817, allowed for "making and maintaining a turn pike from the town of Cromford to the town of Belper". This was promoted by Arkwright Jnr, Hurt and Strutt amongst others who had an interest in making a new and easier route between the two places. A route already existed as a carriage way linking the interests of these three potentates.

The Latinised highway known as the Via Gellia was built on the route of a military road by Philip Gell of Hopton in 1791. This was originally turnpiked in 1804 as it was an important link with Newhaven on the Ashbourne to Buxton turn pike. The original military roadway built by Commonwealth soldiers during the interregnum, to allow their garrison at Soldiers Knoll to race to Nottingham if required. It is said that their leader, the Parliamentary General Sir John Gell, used this energetic exercise to keep his soldiers occupied and less of a menace to the local girls. It was a descendant of these two Gells who gave his name to this road, for Sir William, born in 1777 became a Latin scholar and spent his life writing books about Pompeii and Rome, living in Italy until he died in 1836, he was buried overlooking the Bay of Naples. He was a kind and gentle man who played the guitar, painted and sketched and loved dogs.

Canal

This valley next saw major changes when it was decided to build a canal from Cromford to Langley Mill, a distance of 14 miles (22.5 km) to be named the Cromford Canal. This till exists but is only navigable from Cromford Wharf to and including the Wigwell Aqueduct near to the High Peak Junction.

The need for this was great, for having improved the road access to the village, Arkwright realised that he needed to move heavy loads over long distances. A horse can pull a 25 tonne load on water and only one tonne by cart on a good road, much less on a bad road. For further comparison a pack horse is limited to a load of only 100kg.

James Brindley, Derbyshire born, had already built the Trent and Mersey canal which created a link between Liverpool and Shardlow (sometimes referred to as the Port of Shardlow) – the Clapham Junction of canals – which also connected to Nottingham by the River Trent. Arkwright realised that if he had a canal link with Liverpool, he could buy his raw cotton cheaper due to the lower cost of transport with the possibility of exporting his thread to Lancashire this way. Even more attractive was the thought of sending his thread to the knitters in Nottingham. The canal basin at Langley Mill, the terminal for the Erewash Canal was to become the terminal of the of the Cromford Canal. The Erewash Canal connects with Nottingham.

A meeting held in July, 1788 between the local gentry and industrialists of the area – the Gells of Hopton, Benjamin Outram and Francis Beresford of Butterley, John Wright, Hodgkinson of Ashover and the canal engineer William Jessop. Jessop's credentials were impeccable. His father had worked with John Smeaton, the improver of the water wheel, but had died when his son was sixteen years of age. William was left in Smeaton's care and his pupil worked on the Aire and Calder Canal. Of the promoters, the Gells had interests in lead mining around their estate at Hopton, Outram was a surveyor and engineer in partnership with Beresford, the latter having interests in coal and iron whose works would lie on the route of the canal. John Wright, the grandson of Ichabod Wright, the Baltic Merchant and banker who had helped to finance Arkwright's ventures.

There was opposition from Strutt of Belper and Evans of Darley Abbey. This might have been because the proposed canal may have interfered with their interests.

In 1789/90 an act was passed with amendments in 1791, to allow them to construct a canal, "A navigation from Derby to Cromford, and up the river Amber". The reference to Derby should be noted, because in the event they bye-passed Derby and went to Langley Mill. Had they not done so the canal would have followed the Derwent all the way to Derby to link with the Derby canal. By December of the same year half the estimated £42,697 had been raised with the balance being made available within a further four weeks.

In 1802, Peter Nightingale paid for a branch to be dug to his cotton mill of 1784 at Lea Bridge and his lead smelter near to Lea Bridge. This was and still is known as the Nightingale Arm (and sometimes as the Lea Arm) and is 2.5 furlongs (0.5 km) long. This mill exists, downstream of the original under the banner of John Smedley and Company from 1840 and still makes quality knitwear.

The canal is still provided with sough water, the same water which Arkwright sought for his mill. The sough leat feeds the basin by the warehouse. "Due to the temperature of the Sough Water, the canal remains navigable during severe frost".

As with all canal projects, apparently "insurmountable" obstacles had to be overcome. As this is a history of Cromford, it would be sufficient to deal with the local problems. The canal engineer's nightmare is keeping the canal as level as possible. Changes in level can usually only be dealt with by locks and these waste the time of the user and cost a great deal of money to the promoters. This canal was to proceed along a steep sided Derwent valley and across to Langley Mill, also hilly but less so. The obvious solution was to follow the contour of the hillside from Cromford south to Ambergate.

Part of Burdett's Map of 1791. This shows the river and canal but not the turnpike yet to be built from Cromford to Whatsatndwell (Derbyshiure Archaeological Society)

Act of Parliament for the sale of Cromford Canal.

ANNO NONO & DECIMO

VICTORIÆ REGINÆ.

••

Cap. ccxc.

An Act for authorizing the Sale of the *Cromford* Canal, and other Property of the *Cromford* Canal Company.   [27th *July* 1846.]

WHEREAS an Act was passed in the Twenty-ninth Year of the Reign of His Majesty King *George* the Third, intituled *An Act for making and maintaining a navigable Canal from or from near to* Cromford *Bridge in the County of* Derby *to join and communicate with the* Erewash *Canal at or near* Langley *Bridge, and also a collateral Cut from the intended Canal at or near* Codnor Park Mill *to or near* Pinxton Mill *in the said County,* and certain Persons were thereby incorporated by the Name of the *Cromford* Canal Company, and were authorized to construct and maintain the said Canal and collateral Cut and other Works; and another Act was passed in the Thirtieth Year of the Reign of His Majesty King *George* the Third, intituled *An Act to alter and amend an Act passed in the last Session of Parliament, for making and maintaining a navigable Canal from or from near to* Cromford *Bridge in the County of* Derby *to join and communicate with the* Erewash *Canal at or near* Langley *Bridge, and also a collateral Cut from the said intended Canal at or near* Codnor Park Mill *to or near* Pinxton Mill *in the said County;* and another Act was passed in

29 G.3. c.74.

30 G.3. c.56.

[*Local.*]   56 Y   the

Wheatcroft & Sons Marble Mill at Buckland Hollow. The canvas on the wagon reads - Wheatcroft & Sons. Cromford

The celebrations for the Coronation of King George V on 23 June 1911. The protraits over the cottage window are of the King and Queen, Mary of Teck. The model boat symbolses the King's interest in the Navy, he was called the Salior King. The impact of the bicycle by this date can be seen as can a fine carriage and horse. The shop on the left is the draper next to the Greyhound HOtel and still a shop today. Outram the Currier dressed hides, one hopes that he did not undertake this on the premises!

High Peak Junction. The guard's vans are at the bottom of the Sheep Pasture Incline. Cromford Canal in the foreground (Author)

Leawood Tunnel on the Cromford Canal. Looking south.(Author)

This they did without the use of locks, but other expensive means were necessary in the form of an aqueduct and a tunnel.

The aqueduct takes the canal over the river Derwent close to the Nightingale Arm. The Wigwell Aqueduct is 200 yards (183m) long and 30 feet (9m) at its highest. The two arches over the river have a span of 80 feet (24m) each with an adjoining cattle creep on each side of the main arch. Jessop designed this aqueduct which was constructed between 1792 and 1793. Jessop was not considered to be good with aqueducts, the one at Bull Bridge on the same canal was a source of trouble from its year of completion 1782 on. The one at Wigwell failed for which Jessop blamed the stone he had used, limestone from Crich. He pulled it down and rebuilt it at his own expense and this is the aqueduct we see today.

The Leawood Tunnel, which was driven under Lea Wood still survives and can be walked through. It is brick arched and still in good condition. It has a tow path, therefore boats did not have to "legged" through.

The Wheatcroft family of Cromford were quick to take advantage of the canal. They built and operated barges for the transport of cotton, lead, coal and bricks. The use of Staffordshire blue roof tiles used in the area owes everything to Wheatcroft and the canal. They also leased a transit shed at the canal basin on Mill Lane. To accompany the barges they also had wagons which enabled them to move goods from the canal basin to the customer and vice versa. They did a brisk trade in running fly boats, a small fast passenger carrying craft in which people made day trips to Nottingham.

Problems with the canal started when it was found that the water supply to it was sometimes insufficient. The opening of the Meerbrook Sough at Whatstandwell in 1846 robbed the Cromford Sough of water, which in turn affected the canal. As no other supply could be found permission was obtained for pumping water from the river Derwent into the canal. In 1849, the Leawood Engine was built in a splendid engine house, north of the Wigwell Aqueduct. This engine built by the Milton Ironworks of Graham and Company of Elsecar, is of the Watt single acting bream type having a piston of 5.5 feet (1676mm) diameter and an 8 feet (2438mm) stroke. This drove the pump through a beam having two cast iron plates bolted together and measuring 30 feet (9144mm) long and 4 inches (102mm) thick each. The pump is of the displacement type moving 3.5 tons (3.56 tonnes) of water at a stroke, with 7-10 strokes per minute. By calculation this means that at full rate, this machine could pump up to 470,400 gallons per hour (35,640 litres/m). To remove such quantities of water at times of drought could have caused problems for the users of the river water, the mills downstream, so a stone pad was placed on the river bed under Cromford bridge from which depth measurements would be made. If the water in the river dropped below an agreed level, the pump had to stop. The pump has a bore of 25 inches (635mm) and a stroke of 60 inches (1524mm). The engine power was 90 HP (67kW) and the pump 71HP (53kW). The outlet to the canal is 54 inches (1372mm) diameter and is very impressive when the engine is in steam as water gushes out at 7 strokes per minute into the canal. The present boilers are of the locomotive type for burning coal, built by the Midland Railway Company of Derby, popular with mills at that time.

The engineer who supervised the building of the engine and its house was a one time employee of Richard Trevithick, one John Tretheway, who was active in the area and became a protégé of John Smedley of Lea Mills of hydropathy fame.

The canal suffered mishaps, the worst being the collapse of the Butterley Tunnel in 1889, which was reopened to collapse again in 1903 when it was finally closed. The precursor of British Gas blocked this tunnel at its north end at Bull Bridge.

The canal became the property of the Midland Railway Company in 1852. A case of buying the competition, who let it trade until it became uneconomical. To give some idea of the decline, tonnage carried in 1802/2 was 155,000, by 1850 it was 84,000 and in 1888 it was at an all time low of 45,000 tons.

The wharf was in use in 1872 when it carried coals for sale in the Cromford and Matlock Bath area.

The life of the canal finally came to its end when it was abandoned under the London, Midland and Scottish Railway Act of 1944, bringing about its closure. British Waterways took it over under the Transport Act of 1947, since when it has been the property of Derbyshire County Council and is partly managed by the Arkwright Society of Cromford.

Railways

Manchester, Buxton, Matlock and Midland Junction railway (MBM&MJR)
      later the Midland Railway (MR)
      later the London, Midland and Scottish Railway (LMS)
      later British Rail, Midland Region (BR(M))
      now Central Trains

The advent was not far away. Britain was gripped by railway mania from the 1830s onward. It was only a matter of time before it arrived up the Derwent Valley, to eventually displace the canal as a prime mover of goods and people. Another railway, audacious if not outrageous in its concept from our position in the 21st century, was the Cromford and High Peak Railway (C&HPR).

The railway which came up the valley from Derby and which carried on to Manchester via Buxton arrived at Cromford on 4th June 1849 when it opened to Rowsley from Ambergate and arrived at Manchester in 1867. Before this date, in 1852, the MBM&MJR had entered into a joint lease with Midland Railway for 19 years, Fortunately it ran outside the village thus saving it from the noise, smoke and dust associated with the coal fired steam locomotive. The station of the 1860s which we see today is much as it was built. The whole is in the French style and of some note is the station master's house, all designed by Sir Joseph Paxton's son-in-law, G H Stokes. The line having crossed the flat of the meadows and the river crossing enters the station and then dramatically enters Willersley Tunnel. A lead vain was found when mining this tunnel and this had to be freed by the Barmote Court and duty paid.

The major problem faced by the railway engineer when this line was built was accommodating the existing canal and river. Between Cromford and Ambergate they had to tunnel underneath the canal as well as cross the river, thus adding considerably to the cost of the undertaking which had already sounded the death knell of the canal.

Cromford and High Peak Railway (C&HPR)
    later Midland Railway
    later London, Midland and Scottish railway (LMS)
    later British Rail Midland (BR(M))

The original intention was to link the Cromford Canal with the Peak Forest Canal by a canal over the Pennines. In retrospect this seems a foolhardy idea and was wisely abandoned before it started, common sense prevailing during the period of railway mania. Incredibly other routes were considered for this canal:

    via Tansley, Matlock and Bakewell
    via the Goyt Valley
    via Grindleford, Hope and Edale.

This last proposal was costed at a phenomenal £500,000 (£500 million today) with a prospective revenue of £6,000 per annum!!!

These were all sensibly abandoned at the planning stage. All these schemes suffered from the two problems of too many locks and too little water.

The idea for a railway, equally foolhardy, was put forward in 1814 by Joshua Jessop son of William, the latter being the same man who engineered the Cromford Canal. An Act of Parliament dated 1825 gave progenitors permission to proceed. It was a formidable undertaking and a monument to the ingenuity of those times and represented the ultimate in folly of which this period gave us several examples. The progenitors were Richard Arkwright Jnr. the 6th Duke of Devonshire and Manchester bankers. The Act of Parliament dated 25th May 1825 gave them the go ahead, the estimate for its building was £155,000, the final bill came to £180,000.

To appreciate the problems to be faced one must understand the obstacles to be overcome and the greatest of these was the Pennines themselves. The easiest surveyed route rose from Cromford canal near Cromford to the highest point at Ladman Low (1264 feet, 385m ASL where it is 990 feet (302m) above the canal water level at High

Peak Junction and rises 747 feet (228m) in 8 Miles (13 km) to the Peak Forest Canal at Whalley Bridge. This latter canal, engineered by Benjamin Outram linked the North Derbyshire quarries with Lancashire. When considering such changes in level over a short distance of 33 miles (53 km) it makes one realise how foolhardy a canal would have been, the least of its problems being the need for water and the madness in building a railway over such terrain.

The intention was to undertake the scheme using a wagon-way having horses as the motive power. There were nine inclines, later reduced to eight, where wagons would be hauled by stationary steam engines, the horses taking care of the level stretches. The first four inclines from Cromford lifted the railway by an altitude of 1100 feet (335m) over 5 miles (8 km) – one had to admire their courage. The steepest incline was 1:7 or 14.3%, the remainder averaged 1:14 (7%). In 1877, one of these inclines at Hopton, was eased and one of the stationary engines removed to make it at 1:14 the steepest friction railway in Britain. This was not he only record, for at Gotham, 10 miles (16 km) from Cromford the line curved through 80 degrees in 55 yards (50m) to make it the sharpest bend in the British railway system. The present Sheep Pasture Incline in the parish if Cromford had the benefit of two winding engines, one at the summit level with Black Rocks and the other half way down the incline. The latter was removed in 1857 to make this one incline, a formidable stretch 1300 yards (1190m) long with a gradient of 1:9 (11%) steepening to 1:8 (12.5%) at the top. What an attraction to tourist this would be today. However, in 1888 a wagon filled with limestone broke loose on this incline, jumped the rails at the curve at the bottom, and leapt over the canal and the railway, landing in a field where the sewage works now stands. A catch pit was constructed near to the base of this incline, a little uphill from the A6T.

Work started soon after the act dated 1825 and the work was completed in two parts: Cromford Wharf to Hurdlow on 19th May 1830 and Hurdlow to Whalley Bridge on 6th July, 1831. One can only wonder that such an undertaking should take only 7 years and two months to complete. Stephenson's colliery gauge of 56.25 inches (1430mm) was used throughout. The Butterley Company contracted to supply the engines of which only one survives at Middleton top, near to Middleton by Wirksworth. The original rails were of cast iron with CHPR cast on the sides. These fish belly rails weighed 63lb per yard (26.0 kg/m) and measured 4 feet (1220mm) long.

The first locomotive to replace horses in 1841 was built by Robert Stephenson at Newcastle upon Tyne and was called appropriately the "Peak" and by 1860 all the horses had given way to seven locomotives.

The wagons were hauled up the inclines by means of chains initially, which were replaced in 1855 and 1857 by hemp ropes and four years later by steel wire hawsers or cables. The wagons were limited to 38 tons (38.6 tonnes) fully laden.

Trouble was brewing early. In 1855, there was no dividend for the share holders, debts and interest were overdue. In a desperate attempt to increase revenue, the railway was opened to passenger traffic, something they had not considered on the outset. In the first year they took £4,026 in fares but in 1877, the scheme was abandoned after a passenger was killed on the line, a strange reaction given that from the inception of the railways numerous people were killed on lines and in trains, without having to close the lines.

In its heyday, the line made money by moving lime and stone from the quarries and milk from the farms on the route, as well as water to a few farms. Some of the wagons had to carry water for use by the locomotives.

The line was abandoned in the 1960s and all the metal apart from the engine at Middleton Top was sold for scrap. The Derbyshire County Council with great foresight bought the line, the engine the engine house and the dwelling at Middleton Top along with entire rail bed and together with the Buildings at High Peak Junction. The bed of the line is now the High Peak Trail, enjoyed by many as an amenity, the buildings are interpretive centres.

In this narrow valley we have all the stages of ground transport within a few hundred metres of each other. From east to west we have the old road from Cromford Bridge to Lea, the River Derwent, the railway still in use as far as Matlock (it is now mooted to complete this line to Buxton), the Cromford Canal, the A6T trunk road and the old coach road from Cromford south (Intake Lane).

The Badge of the Cromford and High Peak Railway

Chapter Seven
Buildings

General

The local stone is evident in the local buildings; millstone grit and limestone, both of which were, and are, quarried locally. They have the benefit of durability but with today's costs, they are expensive to work for use as masonry. Millstone was quarried in Cromford, the Barrel Edge Quarry, now picturesquely overgrown on Cromford Moor behind the Black Rocks was used to make millstones and to provide building stone for the village, including possibly parts of Willersley Castle, although Craven and Stanley suggest that it was made from Chatsworth Grit from Oaks Quarry, Blakelow Hill, Tansley.

These grits are a form of sandstone having varying grain sizes from course to fine. Much of the coarser grit was used for walling and the medium grits for housing. It is easily tooled or sawn and was particularly valuable for sturdy cottages and industrial buildings such as the mills. As referred to elsewhere, the stone for Arkwright's first mill came from demolishing Steeple Grange. The advantage to Arkwright would have been the ready cut masonry thus saving him the cost of quarrying and cutting. This grange, once a monastic settlement was at the top of Cromford Hill near to the Cromford and High Peak Railway (now the High Peak Trail).

Limestone was used in the area for walling and some cottages. It is difficult to tool and lends itself more to rough work. Dean Quarry off Cromford Hill is extracting Limestone which is mostly used for road making. This quarry is situated in an area known as Dean Hollow which was extensively mined for lead in the nineteenth century.

The outstanding feature of Cromford Village are its "Arkwright" houses, which line both sides of Cromford Hill and North Street and all built to a standard plan. These were solidly built 1771-76 of the local Gritstone, possibly taken from Barrel Edge Quarry. The original houses built in the 18th century were mostly three storey with a weaving gallery in the top floor. The windows would have been large to admit as much light as possible but many of these have been reduced in size. Also, the window frames were originally of cast iron with many small panes of glass in leaded lights. Some of the later windows were entirely of cast iron, such were being produced by Handyside of Derby in 1873 at 10s to 16s (50p to 80p) per cwt (51 kg) although most of the early window frames were cast at Francis Hurt's foundry at Alderwasley nearby. Fine cast iron work was coming out of foundries in Derbyshire, and only small panes of glass were available at that time due to the casting methods used to make glass. For ventilation they had an inadequate opening in the middle being either slid or tilted to open. Emergency escape through these was impossible. A rare survivor of these windows are at number 9 & 11 (large vents), 31, 37 & 122 (small vents) Cromford Hill.

The houses on North Street - named after Lord North, the then Prime Minister - are fine survivors of the original houses. They stand facing each other over a generously wide road, with the school at the end. These houses are comfortable to live in and would be preferred to many of the houses built today and will probably outlive them too. As well as the traditional three storeys they had cellars too. The whole street was threatened by the local authority who wanted to see them demolished. When the Arkwright Estate was sold off in 1924, these houses passed to the Matlock Urban District Council in 1961 with a view to demolishing them. Derbyshire County Council refused to allow this act of vandalism, for which the old Urban District Council was infamous. Fortunately good sense prevailed over the worst depredations of local government.

Six of these were bought by the Landmark Trust from the Ancient Monuments Society in 1974 who had bought them from the County Council, and six more were bought and all were restored and resold as dwellings bar one. Number 10 is still in the ownership of the Trust together with a paddock and is available for letting as a holiday cottage. It still boasts a cast iron cooking range.

Of Arkwright's cottages Farey wrote, "The cottagers throughout Derbyshire are much better provided with habitations than they commonly are in the Southern Counties of England, and they generally keep them in neat and in better order . . . The vast numbers of neat and comfortable Cottages which have been erected, by the late Sir Richard (Arkwright) and by the present Mr Richard Arkwright, by Messrs Strutts, Mr Samuel Oldknow and numerous others of the Cotton-spinners and Manufacturers, for the accommodation of their multitudes of work-people, must have had a great influence on the general style and condition, now observable in the Cottages." Most of these cottages had an allotment garden and a pig sty, some of which can be seen behind the shops on Cromford Hill and close to the Bear Pit. The gardens are still lovingly tended, the pig sties, solidly built of gritstone are no longer but only a few are intact.

The perennial problem for the houses on Cromford Hill, particularly those on the south-east side is flooding. When the drains on the hill can no longer carry all the water from heavy rain, it flows down the Hill and turns into some of the houses. Slots to take baffle boards can be seen in the door frames of the cottages lower down the hill, to provide a temporary baffle. Originally all such water ran down a gulley at the side of the road and each cottage had its own limestone bridge, polished smooth by thousands of feet and called "marble" bridges for that is how they appeared. This same tradition applied to nearby Bonsall where every cottager was a King who crossed a marble bridge to go home - the commonest names in this village over a century ago were the Kings.

Originally, a row of trees grew down the centre of North street, which must have been helped to reduce the austerity of the houses seen today.

At the far end of North Street can be seen a pipe in the wall and a trough. This was the original water supply for the entire street, being the blocked off portal of Longhead Sough. Today the water is a desultory trickle but there was a time when it gave a plentiful supply. The adage "they who have to carry it know the value of water" would certainly have applied here.

There are numerous old cottages built over the years, some having once been farmhouses. Good examples are Ashes Farm on Intake Lane the farm buildings being on the opposite side of the lane. The Home Farm which provided for Willersley Castle and is situated in the grounds inside the gate to the right was built at the same time. It now provides an annexe to the Castle. Near to the gate can be seen the coach house, tastefully - except for the window shutters - converted into a dwelling. A cottage having mullioned windows on Alabaster Lane which pre-dates Arkwright. A cottage higher up Cromford Hill which also pre-dates Arkwright complete with a lead mine in its back yard. Staffordshire Row at Scarthin is a group of dwellings for workers imported from Staffordshire - which are older than the Arkwright houses having been built in the 1720s.

Victoria Terrace off Cromford Hill built in the 1840s also boasts some good cast iron window frames.

As the village is a conservation area, some of the houses have attracted grants for restoration, under the auspices of the Cromford Town Scheme, notably numbers 95 and 97, Cromford Hill. The roofs are not original and alas they have been reroofed in a mixture of tiles; Staffordshire blue, Marley red, Roman pantile, etc. The original would have been stone (sandstone) slates, Welsh slate arrived after the canal was opened.

Off Cromford Hill are some local authority houses, with single storey dwellings for the old. The newer housing on the corner of Arkwright Gardens is agreeably in keeping with the village as are some multi-storey dwellings on Scarthin - Bakehouse Cottages.
There is an estate of new houses and bungalows, which enjoy panoramic views situated on and off Intake Lane. Alas these are not in keeping with the textures or architecture of the village and from the opposite side of the valley present an eyesore. The author would add that he lives in one of these!

Mills
The cotton mills are covered in chapter four. There are other mills to be seen, which no longer perform as was originally intended. This list does not include mills referred to in Chapter 4.

- Grace Cottage off Mill Lane
- Counting house of 1783/6
- Manager's house by the drive to Rock House off Mill Lane

- the mill at the end of Water Lane on the Scarthin side was where the locally mined barytes was ground to a powder as a base for adding pigment to make paint. The wheel exists, made of cast iron and wrought iron and still turns when there is sufficient water although it no longer turns any machinery. It uses water from the old corn mill opposite and its discharge is into the mill pond. The present owner should be congratulated for putting this over-shot wheel back into turning order after many years of rusting idleness. Trout can be seen in the tail race which also receives water from Alabaster Sough.

- -the site of the original manorial corn mill is opposite the baryte mill. The wheel pit and race can be seen. This is not the original mill but a new mill built by Arkwright for providing flour for the village complete with a drying kiln, store and cottage. The water for this is from the mill pond upstream behind the mill, being a dam on the Bonsall Brook. The discharge water is piped across the road to the baryte mill. It was used in recent times to drive a generator for a motorcycle dealer on Water Lane.

- This mill is on the site of the calamine roasting mill operated during the period 1720-1750. A record left by a visitor in 1746 refers to this mill, "Bellows at these mills are kept in continual motion by running water". The wheel pit housed a 14'9" (4.5m) overshot wheel.

- At the turn of the 19th century the mill was operated by John and Fred Biddulph, father and son. It ceased working in 1935.

- Further up the Via Gellia, on the left at a bend in the road can be seen the roof of Arkwright's bobbin mill, where the machinery is still in existence but in a poor state of repair. This also used the Bonsall Brook. A dilapidated board tells us that this is known as "Slinter Cottage".

Churches and Chapels

The villagers' spiritual welfare was well provided for, for there are, or were a number of churches and chapels which one could attend:

The church of St Mary occupies the site of a lead smelter next to Cromford Bridge. It was commenced before 1792 by Thomas Gardner of Uttoxeter, Staffordshire for use as a family chapel by the Arkwrights. Pevsner tells us that it is similar in design to another Gardner church at Wiggington, Staffordshire. It was complete by 1797, was consecrated in June of that year and was Gothicised in 1858 by Peter Arkwright. The three arched open porch is unusual as is the narrow tower which houses a single bell. The apsidal chancel was added later. The wall paintings- now much spoiled - and the stained glass were by A O Hemming in 1897. The church boasts a monument by Sir Francis Chantry the famous sculpture, born in the county.

Originally the living was with the Arkwright family in the form of the vicarage which was valued at £300 per annum in 1881. It came under the Rural Deanery of Ashover, the Archdeanery of Derby and the Diocese of Lichfield, in Staffordshire. Today it comes under the Diocese of Derby. In 1869, Cromford became an ecclesiastical parish taking areas from Wirksworth, Middleton by Wirksworth Parishes. Scarthin was and still is in the parish of Matlock Bath.

It has some good plate:
>Paten by Thomas Mason, 1732
>Flagon and paton, 1776
>Chalice, 1780
>Chalice and paton cover, 1796

All this plate is kept safely elsewhere.

All bought by Arkwright, the Mason platen being bought second hand except the 1796 chalice which was bought by Richard Jnr. This is now the parish church having stood unused for many years is now coming back into the community again.

The organ is a two manual dating from the 1870s when it was enlarged by Lloyd of Nottingham to make the instrument that we see today. In 1959, Willis enlarged the pedal-board but alas the weather has found its way into the instrument and has wrought some damage, yet to be remedied. The original organ, first recorded in 1824 was located on the gallery as it is today and within four years it was recorded as being "very ill used". It was also recorded that this instrument came originally from Staunton Harold in North Leicestershire having been purchased by Sir Richard Arkwright, probably in May, 1770. This was the organ which was in the church in the grounds of Staunton Harold Hall, one of the few built during the Commonwealth.

The patronal festival of the church is 8th September, the time when Arkwright held the "candle lighting" festival. The register dates from 1797.

It was intended as a private chapel, but Richard Junior opened the church for public worship. He also completed the work started by his father and was endowed by him with £50 per annum later augmented with £200 from him, and £200 from Queen Anne's Bounty and £1000 Parliamentary grant. The tithe was commuted to £63.

- Monuments and memorials are listed in Appendix I.

- The church of St Mark was built in 1877 and comprised a chancel and nave and cost £2,000, on land donated by the Arkwright family, alas we know nothing of this ill fated venture for it fell into disuse in 1957 and was demolished in 1971. The only trace is the graveyard now a cemetery behind the council property off Arkwright Gardens/St Mark's Close. There were no burials at St Mary's for common folk. Prior to 1887, the Cromford dead were interred in the graveyard and the old cemetery at Wirksworth.

- The chapel on Scarthin Promenade overlooking the pond was for the Primitive Methodists and built in 1810 and enlarged in 1853 at a cost of £300. It seated 1,000 worshippers. Saturday schools were held here, boys alternating with girls. It is now a dwelling.

- On the opposite side a footpath apart from Scarthin Books is another chapel of 1912 which replaced a meeting room of 1868. It is now an engineering works. A long and separate room to the rear of the chapel was incorporated for the Wesleyan Reformers or Free Church Methodists.

- On the Via Gellia, facing the old corn mill is yet another chapel of 1912, ruined by a motor repair workshop. This was built in 1868-69 by the vicar of Matlock Bath and his churchwardens to encourage his parishioners from Scarthin to attend for worship. It was called the Scarthin Mission Room. It became redundant and was sold to a Mr and Mrs Gerald Needham, road hauliers, in 1955 for the sum of £400. An application for a canopy and petrol pumps was happily turned down by the local authority.

- The Baptists did not seem to be represented in the village, although it is known that they held services in a building on North Street for some time.

- - Of the chapels built in the area only one survives as a place of worship - the Methodist Chapel and School Room built in 1900 on Water Lane and still in use. Visitors to Willersley Castle use this chapel.

A chapel which has not survived was the Glenorchy Chapel of 1777 built by Arkwright for the Independents and which stood south of Masson Mill. It could seat 300 worshippers. Lady Glenorchy, wife of Viscount Glenorchy, heir to the Earl of Breadalbane was a religious fanatic. In 1785 she was travelling in the area when her carriage broke down. Whilst waiting for it to be repaired she enquired of the state of religion and morals in the area. She did not like what she heard so she bought the chapel with an adjoining house (originally Samuel Need's home) and endowed it as a Congregational Chapel. It boasted an organ, built by Albert Keates of Sheffield in the late 18th century transferred to the Alvaston Congregational Chapel (now the United Reform Chapel) in Derby when the Glenorchy Chapel was demolished to make way for the widening of the A6T in 1951. This organ was replaced by an electronic one in 1995. Lady Glenorchy died the following year at the age of 24. She is remembered by the Glenorchy Centre at Wirksworth. The Revd. T Newnes was pastor from 1831, the father of George Newnes the publisher, founder of "Tit Bits".

- A bridge chapel whose ruins survive by Cromford Bridge. Travellers would light a candle here and beg for a safe crossing through the ford in the river which predated the bridge. Thomas Blackwell of Wirksworth left a fodder of lead toward the maintenance of divine service here. It was mentioned in the will of a Richard Smyth, vicar of Wirksworth who died in 1504 and a Richard Wigley of Middleton by Wirksworth in his will of 1540 left a legacy of 2 shillings (10p) to the "Chappell at Crunford". An inventory of the time of Edward VI refers to "1 vestment and 1 lytle bell without a

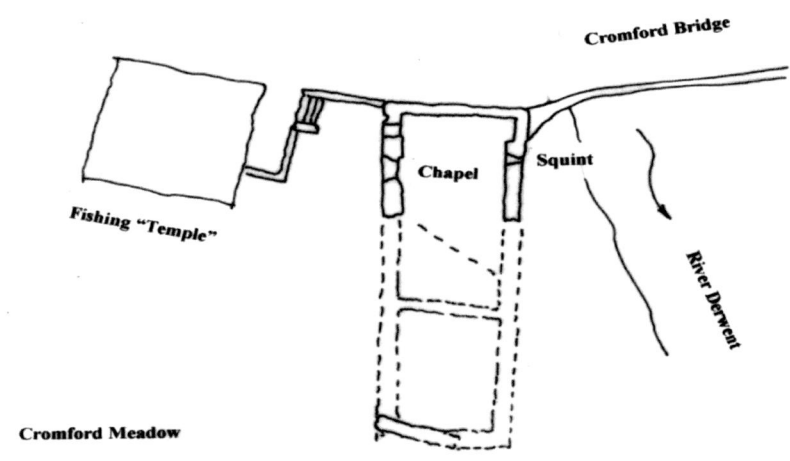

THE BRIDGE CHAPEL
Surveyed by the author, 1996

clapper" at the chapel. A single stained glass window displayed the arms of Lord Talbot. The priest who took care of this building and the worshippers was paid out of the offerings of the travellers. After the Reformation, it was used as a dwelling house being pulled down in 1796 by Richard Arkwright Jnr for reasons unknown.

Hotels and Inns

Greyhound Hotel - built by Arkwright in 1790 on the site of the Black Dog Inn, as a resting place on the Ashbourne to Chesterfield Turnpike and as a lodging for his many visitors and as a stabling for the Manchester coach. Built solidly in a town hall style, it still boasts a clock and a fine elevation overlooking the market place, which fortunately has not changed over its two hundred years. It is built from millstone with limestone quoins and window frames. The entrance is a fine Georgian one. When the Honourable John Byng stayed in June, 1790 he recorded it as "cheap and pleasant with good stabling".

The Boat Inn on Scarthin Promenade predates Arkwright. A lintel over one door proclaims the date 1772 but parts are older. This farmhouse style building is of millstone grit.

The Bell Inn at the corner of North Street and Cromford Hill is of local brick and millstone the latter dating from the time of the building of North Street.
The Rutland Arms – now demolished stood near to the Glenorchy Chapel.

King's Head - a three storied Georgian inn, now demolished stood near to the Glenorchy Chapel, see above. It was originally the dwelling of Needs the manager of the Masson Mill.

The Cock Inn – stood at the corner of North street and Cromford Hill (now numbers 43 & 45 Cromford Hill) on the opposite corner to the Bell Inn

School

Built by Richard Junior in 1832 it had provision for boys in a building on one side of a square court and girls on another side, with separate residences for a schoolmaster and a schoolmistress. All have survived but have been modified. By 1881, the school had 220 children on its role! Happily the school is still in use for the village children under much less cramped conditions. This is a Church of England aided school.

Willersley Castle

Built 1789-90 of Millstone Grit from Oakes Quarry, Blakelow Hill, Tansley, to designs by William Thomas of London 1789-90, when it was burned down due to the carelessness of a workman. It was built for Arkwright in revivalist gothic but he died before he could occupy it. His son Richard finished it using a different architect, Thomas Gardner of Uttoxeter.

The platform was cut from solid rock and this alone cost £3,000. The total cost came to £20,000 which probably includes the rebuilding, insurance was not easily available in those days.

The Honourable John Byng called it "an effort of inconvenient ill Taste" and "It is the house of an overseer surveying the works, not of a gentleman . . . .Sir Richard has honourably made his great fortune: and so let him live in a great cotton mill!", Pevsner was kinder, "entirely classical in conception, but romanticised by battlements" and he considered the best feature to be the oval hall, "with galleries on both upper storeys, a skylight". One cannot dispute him. As we do not know what this house looked like when Byng was reporting in June, 1790, we must accept that perhaps his judgement might have been correct, we were possibly saved this "ill taste" by a fire.

Today, it sits square against the valley that Arkwright transformed, facing the deserted lead smelting village of Willersley and with the River Derwent racing at the foot of the field which acts as a lawn to the house. It looks fine sitting amongst the numerous trees, planted by Richard Junior, who did have the pleasure of living in it. By 1924 it was empty, when the estate was sold. In 1948 the Methodist Guild Holiday organisation bought it and are still in occupancy. During this new life it has given numerous people the chance of a rest in a fine house in beautiful surroundings, for the outlook from the windows on the front is unequalled anywhere and it sits in a superb pleasure ground with many mature trees. One of these latter was a Gosseberry Tree, which in 1857 was 30 feet (9m) high with branches spreading 365 feet (111m).

It is Grade II listed. The Millstone Grit is of the Chatsworth series. The flat roof is of lead.

A door in a wall to the north of the house gives private access to Lovers' Walks, Hag Tor and Wild Cat Tor.

Rock House

This was Arkwright's first home in Cromford and was his home until he died, having been cheated at the last minute from living in his Willersley Castle.. Well named for it stands on a rocky bluff looking down onto his mill yard. It is an imposing building of Millstone Grit and is complete with stables and a coach house. It has had mixed fortunes and is now split into flats and houses have been built in the grounds.

Frances Arkwright the unmarried daughter of Richard Arkwright Junior lived here with a companion and seven servants. She later moved to Oakhill. In the 1861 census return it was uninhabited.

Prior to Arkwright it was occupied by the Curzon family and by a Strutt.

Talk of a tunnel connecting this house with the mill to permit Arkwright unheeded access can safely be discounted.

Cromford Bridge Hall or Bridge House

Built of Carboniferous Limestone and Millstone Grit it was started in 1642 by Henry Wigley, the eighth son of Henry Wigley of Wigwell, Wirksworth Moor. It is Jacobean in design. It passed to Millicent Wigley, an heiress of Anthony Wigley in 1684 and then to a Samuel, son of John Spateman of Road Nook, who Georgianised it. It was sold to George, third son of Edmund Evans of Winster. His son, by the heiress of Peter Nightingale of Lea Hall died in 1769 leaving it to a co-heiress who gave it to her son W E Nightingale. It was occupied by another sister, Elizabeth until she died "very old" in the 1890s. (The author acknowledges the work done by Craven and Stanley for this information). Early in the 19th century it was occupied by the Crompton-Evans family, founders of modern banking.

The house is still a private residence, part of it being operated as a nursery school.

It is Grade II listed. The Millstone Grit is of the Ashover Series. The roof is of stone slates.

Cromford Court

This very fine looking building of 1910, stands high off the main A6 road, facing Masson Mill. It was built by a Mr Laughton, a barrister, as a residence and as legend has it, a fit and proper place to raise his many daughters from where he intended they should marry into the local gentry. This ambition he achieved and made himself bankrupt in the process. It is a beautifully designed and built gentleman's residence and sits well on a platform cut out of the hillside, surrounded with numerous mature trees.

A grape vine carved in sandstone surrounds the main door with each daughter's initials carved on a separate leaf, the intention being to add the groom's initials after each marriage.

After Laughton's time, the house had a varied existence, one being as a preparatory school. In 1978 it was offered by the then owner, Mr Dolphin to the writer for £40,000 complete with numerous acres of woodland. It was bought by the New Tribes Mission who restored it and used it as their headquarters. At the time of writing it stands empty.

Vicarage

The fine millstone vicarage is located off a private drive which links Intake Lane with North Street. It is now occupied by a computer company who have placed a pool in the lawn as a heat sink for computer hardware.

Alison House

Alison House, originally Oakhill House (or Oakhill) was built circa 1845 for a branch of the Arkwright family. In 1851, the Reverend G Henry Arkwright, the Rector of Heath and Ault Hucknall lived here with five servants. He was the son of Peter Arkwright. Frances Arkwright was living here with a companion and four servants having moved from Rock House.

It then became a dower house for the Arkwright family until it was sold in 1924 with the rest of the estate. It was then occupied by the new estate owner and his wife, Mr and Mrs Stanley Key. Following this the occupants were Mr and Mrs Chislett, he being a professional chellist who wrote for the magazine "The Gramophone". In 1967 it was bought by a trust on behalf of the Womans' Association of the Toc-H movement, founded by a nurse in World War I, Alison McPhee, hence its present name..

It is now a conference centre for the Toc-H movement.

The Ashes (now Ashes Farm)

This farm house sits to the east of Intake Lane with its barn and other buildings across the lane.

Bede Houses

The Bede Houses – old references refer to these as a hospital - situated on Bedehouse Lane off Cromford Hill were endowed by Dame Mary Talbot in her will of 1662 which left money for the purchase of land and the erection of the houses. These were intended for six elderly and poor widows or widowers. They had a rent charge of £16.50 per annum from the manor – she was the Lady of the Manor – but by Arkwright's time this was reduced to £14 p.a. Each resident received 40 shillings (£2.00) per annum and 6s 8p (33p) at Christmas towards the purchase of a gown. Mr James Arkwright paid 5s (25p) per week to each resident out of the income from £2,500 invested in 4% Midland Railway debenture stock. From this the trustees were required to pay between 5s (25p) and 6s (30p) to each of the six residents, the surplus to be "given to deserving and necessitous inhabitants of Cromford".

They are now private residences.

Fishing Lodge

A small square stone built fishing lodge, now restored, stands by Cromford Bridge with "Piscatorium Sacrum" cut in Gothic script in a lintel. This is similar to the fishing lodge by the River Dove in Beresford Dale and may be a copy of it. It was restored in 1968.

Lady Armine's Bede House with the now rare stone slate roof. (Author)

The Cock Inn (Author)

Arkwright Houses on North Street (P.J. NAYLOR)

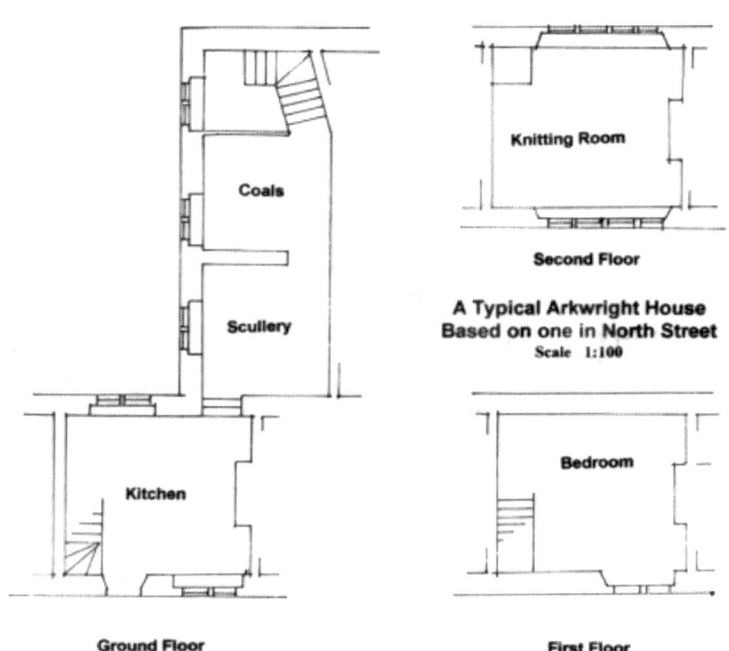

**A Typical Arkwright House
Based on one in North Street**
Scale 1:100

Market Place

The original market placed where Arkwright's market was held lies in front of the Greyhound Hotel. The stone built stalls backing onto Scarthin Promenade were once open fronted and were used by butchers originally and stall holders selling locally grown produce later. These are now closed in and are used by a sandwich bar, video loan shop, fish and chip shop and a store. The market place is now a car park, under which runs the culvert carrying the water from the pond behind the hotel to the mills. The first market was held on 19 June 1790 and failed due to competition from Wirksworth, Belper and Matlock.

Working Mens' Institute

This is on Cromford Hill facing North Street. Note that there was no womens' equivalent. This was given by Peter Arkwright and originally comprised a reading room and meeting room. It was and to some degree still is the village hall.

Note the absence of vehicular traffic and the empty Market Place. The village blacksmith is open for business, the field above Water Lane is empty of buildings.

An Arkwright house on Cromford Hill with its original cast iron window frames.   (P.J. Naylor)

A sketch of Scarthin c.1850

Working Mens' Institute (Author)

The Vicarage (P.J Naylor)

Head Teacher's House (Author)

Cromford School (Author)

Chapter Eight
Cromford apart from the Arkwrights

If ever a village was dominated by one family it was, Cromford.

The influence of the originator of the Arkwright dynasty left a lasting and enduring impression. Although there is no representative of the family in Cromford today, their presence is still felt. The mills are a tourist attraction and to a lesser extent so is the village. Any term weekday will find at least one school party undertaking a project with a teacher in charge to explain the details to look for, the houses, the sough portal, the hill, market place, et al.

However, it would be unreasonable to assume that cotton spinning was the only industry in Cromford in the nineteenth century. The large - by the standards of the day - village needed to be supported by supportive trades. In its heyday of 1841 it is interesting to note the various trades in practice:

Mills and associated professions

Cotton carders	2	
Cotton spinners	131	including one aged 70 and 72, and one aged 10
Engineer	1	the engine minder
Frame work knitters	10	mostly on North Street
Mechanics	9	including an apprentice, these were to become known as millwrights.
Silk throwster	1	a mystery this, were they experimenting with silk at the mill?
Tin plate worker	1	
Weavers	7	
Wood Tuner	1	used for building throstles

Transport

Blacksmiths	12	some of these would be working in the mill
Boatmen	18	including a 9 year old and 6 in barges
Brush maker	1	
Carriers	6	
Engine tenters	2	
Ostlers	2	
Road surveyor	1	
Sadler	1	
Toll collectors	2	one aged 15!
Wheelwrights	2	

Building

Carpenter	2	
Joiner	14	including one who was also a publican and an apprentice
Marble Masons	9	
Mason	8	
Painter		1
Plater	1	
Plumber and Glazier	1	
Sawyer	2	
Stone cutter	1	

Services

Bakers	7	
Barber	1	
Basket maker	1	
Butchers	3	
Coal merchants or dealers	2	
Confectioner	1	
Coopers	2	
Drapers	2	
Dress makers	6	
Druggist	1	
Grocers	9	
Hatters	30	including a manufacturer
Millers		3
Milliners	2	
Paste maker	1	
Post boys	2	
Publicans victualler	9	including one aged 80, one who was also a joiner and a
Shoe makers	28	including cordwainers and a manufacturer aged 27
Tailors	15	

Lead Mining

Miners	49	including one aged 80 and another 85

Farming and estate

Farmers	12	
Game keeper	1	
Gardeners	6	
Servants	9	Richard Arkwright II family at Willersley
	14	Peter Arkwright family at Rock House

Other

Artist	1	
Attorney's clerk	1	
Clock maker	1	
Comb maker	1	
Drip makers	2	a mystery profession?
Merchants	2	
Ministers	2	
Nail cutters	1	
Paper makers	15	including a manufacturer
Petrifactioner	1	
Rope maker	1	
Seaman	1	a long way from the sea!
Spectacle maker	1	
School masters and Mistresses	7	this includes those at the Glenorchy Chapel
Solicitor	1	
Spar turner	1	
Watchman	1	

Where else would one find a petrifactioner other than in Matlock Dale, where the petrifying qualities of the local springs, mostly warm, were used to turn anything from hats to birds nests into stone. The same process produces Tufa which was quarried locally to provide Victorians with stone for their grottos.

At this time and for long after Cromford had both a hat factory and a shoe factory. The manufacture of hats was based on the numerous rabbits to be found in the area, a tradition that lived on from the warrens of Sir Hugh de Meynell in the thirteenth century. The warrens were located on Cromford Moor, where the forest now stands, operated by the Wigwell Estate. Further rabbit skins would have been bought from game keepers and the like. The shaved skins, coated with shellac made a semi-hard hat beloved of most working men but especially by agricultural workers, bargees and miners, for they afforded protection against rain or falling water, and when stuffed with grass made an effective safety hat. They were known locally as Bradder Beavers, for the best of these were reputably made in Bradwell higher up the county. This factory still stands for it became a school room to the adjacent chapel.

Shoe manufacture was also a local industry which relied on the skins of locally slaughtered cattle. The location of the factory is not known if there was one, shoe making - and by definition boot making - was probably a cottage industry.

Of further interest are the references to the following:

- The skills required at the mill are obvious. What is not so obvious is the relatively low number of cotton spinners at 131. The remainder must have come in from adjoining parishes, Matlock, Bonsall, Wirksworth and further afield.

- One would also expect more frame work knitters or stockingers. This ties in with a serious depression in this trade, hosiery by now was being undertaken on new and faster machines.

- The number of boatmen is to be expected where a village also boasted a canal terminus. The Cromford Canal was active at this time, the railway had yet to arrive.

- The toll collectors were at the toll bar near to Masson Mill.

- Nine marble masons and one spa turner are an indication of a prosperous cottage industry in the area of working Derbyshire marbles, not true marbles but varieties of dense limestone which would take a polish, eg: black marble from Ashford in the Water, Rosewood Marble from a mine in Shacklow Wood, Sheldon and fossiliferous marble from Ricklow Quarry in Lathkill Dale near to Monyash.

- The plumber also did the glazing, for early glass had to be mounted in leaded lights and relied on the skills of a plumber.

- They must have consumed a large amount of bread with seven bakers to make it.

- The number of publicans could be misleading, for there were many beer houses as well as inns, where the innkeeper would have had a second job. Lead mining and agricultural work were popular with these people.

   The names of the public houses at this time were:

Cock	near to Masson Mill
Bell Inn	still with us
Bulls Head	now the Boat Inn
Greyhound Hotel	still with us

   Later in the century, after the advent of the railways we would add:

Junction	on the main road near to High Peak Junction
Railway Inn	somewhere near to the rail station

- The prosperity of the lead mines at this time is reflected by the 49, all male, miners.

- The paper makers all worked at the paper mill next to Masson Mill.

- The drip maker remains a mystery! A tallow candle maker?

Some Cromford people moved away and made new lives for themselves. Space would not permit us to delve too deeply into this subject, but one particular lady, Cromford born and bred stands as a typical example. Mary Barton was born in Cromford in 1829 and by all accounts she was an attractive woman. Her mother was an Allen of Cromford, which family was prosperous locally, the same family which gave its name to Allen Hill which overlooks the Market Place from the south. Her maternal grandmother was a Wolley of Bonsall and a direct descendant of the Wolleys of Riber Hall.

On Boxing Day, 1857, she married a William Gell of the Bell Inn on Cromford Hill at Matlock Parish Church, for she was living at that time in Scarthin of that parish. Three years later she was a widow for poor William died on 12th October of that year of "consumption and heart failure". At that time he was working for his father-in-law, Thomas Barton, draper, whose shop was adjacent to the Greyhound Hotel overlooking the market place (it is still a shop).

Mary along with her sister Elizabeth, emigrated to the United States of America in 1852 along with the latter's husband Joseph Herrod. Meanwhile a John Burton of Bonsall had already made Mary's acquaintance. Burton along with his two brothers had already emigrated to the States where they had put knowledge gained when lead mining at Bonsall to good use and had become prosperous miners, smelters and merchants in Dubuque County, Iowa. John Burton had already met Mary when visiting Bonsall in 1852 and it would appear that he was strongly attracted to her, an attractive widow of six months. They appear to have come to an arrangement whereby she would go to the States and on arrival marry John.

This she did, giving the cause for her first husband's death as having been killed as a soldier fighting in the Afghan Wars. There were no such wars, he had died in bed in Cromford. This was obviously used as a ruse to avoid being denied entry into the States on the grounds that she too could have "consumption". The man who became her second husband was already sick and ailing, he was 57 years, easily old enough to be her father. He was also very rich.

Mary became a rich widow and was still young and attractive. Her third husband was General Samuel Mountford Stokley, she was widowed again and her fourth husband was a kinsman of her third, one Judge Thomas Stokely Wilson who she divorced for he was an alcoholic. Each of her three last marriages added to her wealth, this along with inheriting property in Scarthin, made her a very rich woman indeed. She was 32 years of age! It was said that she was one of the largest land owners in the state of Iowa. She was present at the nomination of Abraham Lincoln as President of the United States in Chicago, Illinois prior to his being elected president in 1861.

The Joseph Herrod who married Mary's sister hailed from Manchester but became a cotton spinner in Arkwright's mill. He became Mary's agent and confessed on his death bed that he had swindled her. Mary is buried in Linwood Cemetery, Dubuque, Iowa and her head stone carries a memorial to her first husband, William Gell, who also has a memorial over his true grave in the churchyard at St Giles, Matlock. He therefore has the rare distinction of having a memorial on both sides of the Atlantic Ocean. William was descended from a cadet branch of the Gells of Hopton.

This story reads like fiction and is a rare example, but many did leave the area to seek and find their fortunes elsewhere. Many emigrated to the new world and the colonies, particularly the lead miners who were expert in hard rock mining. Derbyshire names can be found where ever there are mines in the world as well as in Wales and Scotland.

Of all the well known names which were born in or near to Cromford, Alison Uttley is probably the one that springs to mind. She was born Alice Taylor at Castle Top Farm on the east facing hill overlooking Cromford Meadows where she spent her youth. She tells in her writings of a Cromford long gone, of an age when the motor car was new and the dependence on the railway for escaping and the reliance on village stores, bakers and drapers. She achieved fame by writing those delightful stories for children having unforgettable characters such is Little Grey Rabbit, all as good if not better than Beatrix Potter and in a similar mould. For this alone she is immortalised but she should also be remembered for introducing to us a warm and gentle story of the village of long ago and must go down in the annals of women's fight for equality by being one of the first women to obtain an honours degree in physics. Her writing started in 1928 and her husband James Uttley, took his own life two years later. Her writing must have been both a source of income and a comfort to her, especially after her son also took his own life. She died in 1976 the year of the long hot summer, she was born in the winter snows of 1884.

The village of Alison Uttley carried on into the 1920s, still under the patronage of the Arkwright family. The big turning point was when the estate was sold in 1924, thus opening the door to developers. At the time of the sale of the estate, the mills were given over to the Cromford Colour Company, The Troy Laundry (Mrs May) and Hill's Brewery (later taken over by Offilers of Derby). Mr Taylor of Castle Top Farm – Alison Uttley's father – bought his farm as a sitting tenant having paid a rent of £61 per annum for his 38 acres (94 hectares). A further 1136 acres (2,807 hectares) of land and many farms and houses fell under the hammer on 13th and 14th March 1924 at the New Bath Hotel, the sale having been ordered by Captain R Arkwright. There is little evidence of change until the 1930s when some houses were built, the biggest changes have been post Second World War, evidenced by new housing both private and local authority, especially that rash of building off Intake Lane.

The whole village was alarmed and shocked by the cold blooded murder of a young couple on Easter Sunday, 15th April, 1979. Lorraine H Underwood, aged 15 of Cromford was battered to death, her boy friend who was with her, Peter K Thompson aged 18 was shot to death. Later a local man surrendered to the Police and admitted his crime. Everyone in and close to the village felt this very keenly, the writer well remembers being questioned by the police as were all males in the area. Lorraine would have been 37 years of age at the time of publication – she could have been the mother of children in their teens

On a happier note, Silas Marner was filmed in the area and it is interesting to note the locations as the film moves from scene to scene. This was appropriate, for the author, George Eliot, author of the book of the same name, new Cromford well. She visited her uncle and aunt at Wirksworth regularly and she modelled many of her books on the area and its people.

Another writer, D H Lawrence of Eastwood, Nottinghamshire knew the area well and for two years lived at Mountain Cottage overlooking the Via Gellia, Middleton by Wirksworth. His mother was a Beardsley from Middleton and he referred to the area in his letters to Katherine Mansfield.

Many changes have been witnessed, the opening up of the cutting through Scarthin Nick to make the A6T wider in 1951 The introduction of traffic lights at the crossing of the A6T by the road from the village to Mill Lane, the infill housing in the grounds of Rock House and the conversion of the house into flats. The encroachment of Dean Quarry into the fields in an area once known as the Dean which was heavily mined for lead. The selling for scrap of the old Cromford and High Peak Railway and its adaptation as a thoroughfare for leisure use with a car park and toilets at the site of the old Cromford Moor Mine and High Peak Junction.

The essentials are still there: there is still a baker in the village, the smithy is given over to a health and beauty parlour and the village can boast the real "Arkwright's Store", a name made famous by a television comedy series.

The geography and the planning acts will prevent any further expansion and will ensure that any alterations will be undertaken sensitively. Already we can see the benefit of these constraints by the new local authority housing on Scarthin Promenade and at the junction of Cromford Hill and Arkwright Gardens, built from local stone and in a local vernacular.

The quarrying prospers, lead mining is only a memory, the heritage industry succeeds where the cotton mills have failed, people walk and ride on the bed of a railway which was doomed before it started and the canal is now an amenity where once the horses laboured at pulling barges filled with coal, cotton, straw and lead. There are times when it would be a delight to be a fly on the wall and see the village as it was in Arkwright's time and before.

APPENDIX I
Monuments and Memorials - St Mary's Church

Inside the church
There are ten pointed Gothic arches, five on each side of the apse, made of local sandstone of which eight carry white marble inserts engraved as follows (counting in a clockwise direction):

1. Frederic C Arkwright Esq. of Willersley only son of Frederic Arkwright born 7th November 1853 died July, 18th 1923 and Rebecca Olton his wife, daughter of Sir John Gay Alleyne, born 20th June 1860 died 9th March 1944

2. Richard Arkwright Esq. of Willersley only son of Sir Richard Arkwright born 19th December 1755 died 23rd April 1843 Mary his wife, daughter of Adam Simpson of Bonsall born 6th August, 1755 died 24th February, 1827
   Their daughters:
   Mary   died 9th July, 1803 aged 15 years
   Harriet   died 7th November, 1815 aged 17 years
   Frances   born 23rd August, 1796   died 4th November, 1863

3. Peter Arkwright Esq of Willersley 3rd son of Richard Arkwright born 17th April, 1784 died 19th Sept 1866
   Mary Ann his wife daughter of Charles Hurt of Wirksworth, born 17th March, 1786 died 6th September, 1872

4. Sir Richard Arkwright Knight founder of this church born Preston, Lancs 23rd December, 1732 died 3rd August 1792

5. Frederic Arkwright Esq of Willersley eldest son of Peter Arkwright born 16th August, 1806 died 6th December 1874
   Susan Sabrina his wife daughter of Venerable Archdeacon Burney born 25th February, 1818 died 7th October 1874

6. vacant

7. Richard A Arkwright elder son of Frederic C Arkwright of Willersley born 1st September, 1884 died 29th April 1965
   Marjorie his wife daughter of Frank Hardcastle born 12th March, 1888 died 15th February 1965

8. Frederic George Alleyne Arkwright younger son of Frederic C Arkwright Captain XI Hussars and the Royal Flying Corp killed on duty when flying Nr Montrose N.B. 14th October 1915 aged 29 years
   also his brother-in-law and best friend Guy Bonham-Carter 3rd son of Alfred Bonham-Carter CB Captain XIX Hussars Adjutant Q O (Queens Own) Oxfordshire Hussars he was killed in action near Ypres, 14th May, 1915 aged 30 years

9. Colonel Peter Arkwright 11th Hussars (Prince Albert's Own) eldest son of

Richard Arkwright born 2nd April, 1913 at Willersley Castle died 16th November 1987

10. vacant

Footnote:
the Arkwright tradition spelled Frederic without the final k
the Frederic who died in 1915 appears on memorials to the dead of World War I located both in the church and on the village memorial
the additions in parenthesise are by the writer

There are two sculptured memorials, mounted on black slate panels and hung on the church walls as follows:

♦ South wall of the nave adjacent to the chancel arch:

Charles Arkwright Esq. of Dunstall, Staffs
5th son of Richard Arkwright of Willersley,
Born 22nd Novr 1786, Died 28th Decr 1850
Also Mary his wife
Daughter of Edward Sacheverel Wilmot Sitwell of Stainsby House
Born 6th Decr 1788, Died 29th Novr 1858
(sculpted - H Week ARA 1859)

♦ North Wall of the nave adjacent to the chancel arch:

Martha Maria wife of Richard Arkwright Junr Esqr
Daughter of Revd William Beresford of Ashbourne
rd:died 12th March 1820 aged 40 years
Richard Arkwright died 19th November, 1810   aged 5 weeks
Richard Arkwright died 18th February, 1813   aged 6 weeks
Agnes Maria Arkwright died 16th March, 1813   aged 4 years
(sculpted - Sir Francis Chantry)

below which is a separate white marble plaque:

Richard Arkwright Junr
of Normanton Turville, Leics.
Eldest son of Richard Arkwright of Willersley
born 30th September, 1781
died 28th March 1832

♦ In the naive:

Brass plaque - Frank Smith verger and sexton died October 16th 1953

Brass plaque - Augustus Peter Arkwright, Commander Royal Navy
7th son of Peter Arkwright of Willersley
represented North Derbyshire in Parliament 1868-1880

died 6th October 1887 aged 66

- Stone plaque forming the sill of the second window from the chancel arch with arms and crest and motto "MULTA TULI PECIQUE"

  Frederic Charles Arkwright JP DL of Willersley
  49 years Squire of Cromford
  born 7th November, 1853 died 18th July 1923
  tablet erected by his neighbours and friends

- Brass plaque:
  George Arthur Hazlehurst
  Vicar of Cromford 1915-40
  Rural Dean of Wirksworth
  Honorary Canon of Derby Cathedral
  died 14th December, 1940

- Brass plaque - This church was restored and decorated to commemorate the centenary 1897-8
  Egbert Hacking   Vicar
  F C Arkwright   )
  H Wheatcroft   ) Churchwardens

- Brass plaque -   Frank Smith   verger 1906-1933
                    sexton 1916-1933
                    died 16th October 1933 aged 59

- Brass lectern: James Charles Arkwright, born 1st October, 1813 died 16th May 1896

- Bible - inscribed on fly leaf: In memory of Eileen Stone 20.2.1930 - 9.4.1988

- Brass plaque on the book rest, front pew:
- To the fond memory of Beatrice Boden - a regular worshipper at this Church died 1986.

In the entrance porch:

- Brass plaque - list of men who died during World War I (the Great War 1914-18)
  Framed and glazed - list of the men of Cromford who fought in World War I (served in the King's forces)

Memorials in the Churchyard

- James Charles Arkwright
  died 16th May 1896 aged 82 years
  Mary Esther widow of died 8th February 1918 aged 92 years
  "until the daybreak and the shadows flee away"

Song of Solomon Chapter 2 verse 17

- Emily Elizabeth Arkwright born 6th July, 1847 died 28th March, 1923

- Florence Arkwright 1856-1948
    "When morning gilds the skies,
    my heart awakening cries
    May Jesus Christ be praised"

- Richard Alleyne Arkwright born 1st September, 1884 died 29th April, 1965
  Marjorie daughter of Frank Hardcastle his wife born 12th March, 1888 died 15th February 1965

- Frederic Charles Arkwright born 7th November, 1853 died 18th July, 1923
  Rebecca Olton his wife, daughter of Sir John Gay Alleyne
  born 20th June 1860 died 9th March 1944

- Frederic George Alleyne Arkwright
    Captain XI Hussars and Royal Flying Corp
    died when flying on duty 19th October 1915
        "Steadfast and true - Per Ardua ad Astra"

Stained Glass in the Church

The chancel glass was installed in 1897-8 to commemorate the anniversary of the Church. All the stained glass was by A O Hemming of 47, Marjorie Street, Cavendish Square, London at a cost of approximately £1000 plus public subscriptions. There are three such windows having six glazed panels - each window has two panels divided by a stone mullion.

The subjects are - north to south:

1. The Agony in the garden
2. Christ bearing the Cross
3. The Crucifixion
4. The Resurrection
5. The Charge to St Peter - "Feed my Sheep"
6. The Descent of the Holy Ghost

- Over these are the symbols of the Three Persons of the Trinity: the Hand (of the Creator), the Lamb (the Redeemer) and the Dove (the Comforter)

- The north-east nave window, by artist unknown, is dedicated: "Give thanks to God for the beloved memory of Henry Wheatcroft, Churchwarden of this Parish 1886 to 1912 who died May 14th 1912 aged 56 years. His wife dedicates this window AD 1913

- The three windows over the altar are dedicated thus:

- Frederic Arkwright died 1874
- Janes Charles Arkwright died 1896, made 1897
- Fanny Jane Galton died 1894 the centenary of the church.

War Memorials   Refer to Appendix VIII

St. Mary's Church, Cromford

Footnote:
The writer is indebted to the Parochial Church Council for allowing access to the church on a fine late summer's evening. This is a lovely church and it now looks as if the much needed funds are being made ready for the badly needed restoration this place of worship and haven of peace deserves.

APPENDIX II
A Pedigree of the Arkwright Family

Names marked * have memorials outside the church of St Mary, Cromford
Names marked # have memorials inside the church of St Mary, Cromford

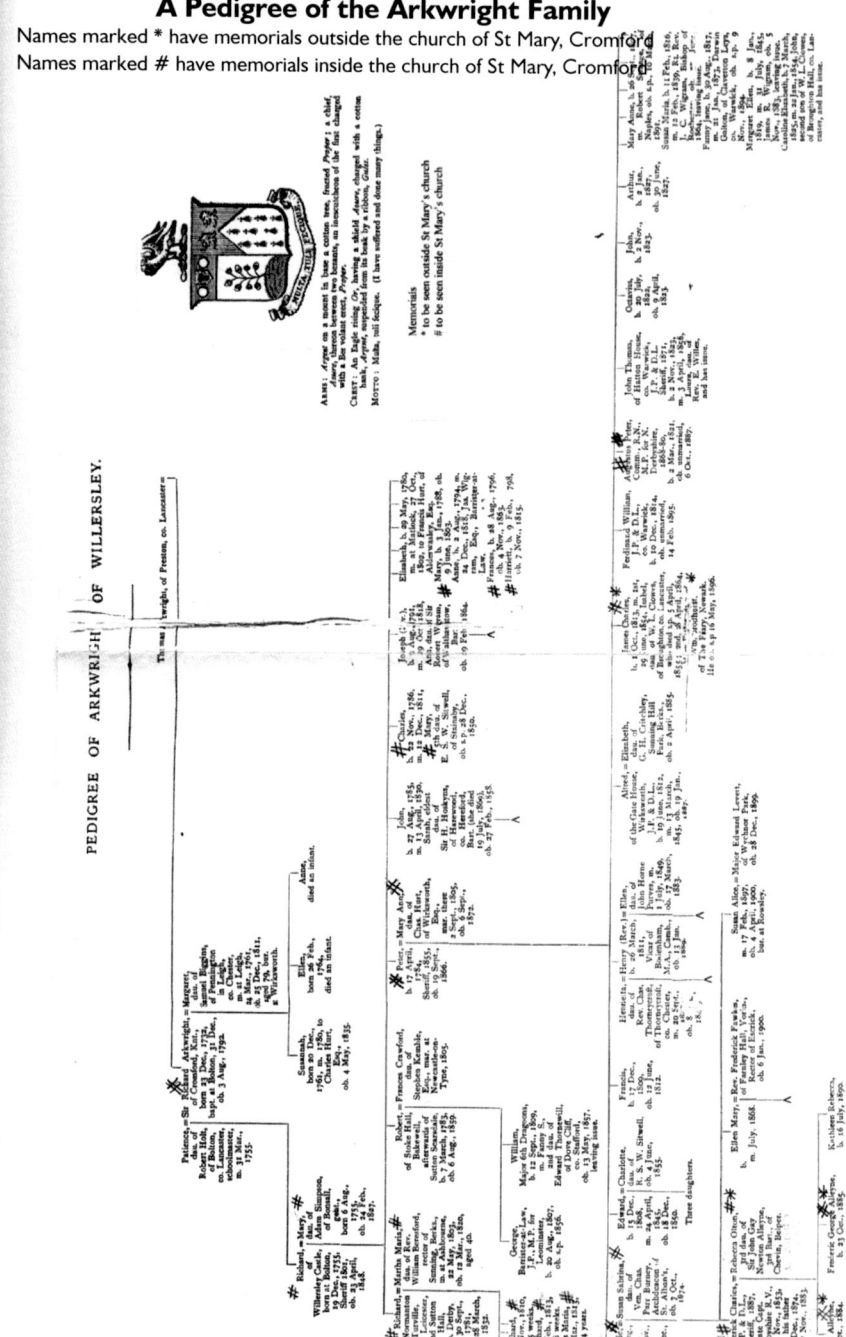

APPENDIX III
A Pedigree of the Hurt Family

Pedigree of HURT, of Ashbourn, Alderwasley, Wirksworth, &c.

ARMS of Hurt. A shield quarterly. 1 Hurt. *Sable*, a fesse between three cinquefoils, *Or*. 2 Lowe. *Gules*, a Wolf passant, *Argent*. 3 Lowe. *Azure*, a Hart trippant, *Argent*. 4 Fawne, *Argent*, a Bugle, *Sable*, between three crescents of the last, each charged with a besant.
CREST of Hurt. A Hart passant, *Proper*, attired, *Or*, hurt or wounded in the flank with an arrow of the second feathered, *Argent*.
MOTTO. Mane predam vesperi spolium.

Thomas Hurt —

William Hurt, of Ashbourn = Joan, dau. of —— Leigh, of Mathsfield.

Thomas Hurt, of Ashbourn = Ellen, daughter of Richard Wright, of Darbie.

Tho. or Christ. H. of Ashbourn = Ellen, daughter of Thomas Blackwall, of Shirley.

Thomas Hurt, of Ashbourn = Mary, daughter of Rauf Gell, of Hopton.
This line ended in an heiress who married a Byrom.

Nicholas Hurt, of Ashbourn and Kniveton. — Ralph Hurt, ancestor of Hurt, of Bristol.

Thomas Hurt, ancestor of Hurt of Kniveton. — Roger Hurt, of Casterne, co. Stafford, younger son. = Edith, dau. of John Cookaine, of Baddesley, co. Warwick, buried 1589.

Nicholas Hurt, born 1567, living at Biore, co. Stafford, 1612, obt. 1647, had four sons and three daughters. = Helen, dau. of John Berresford, gent. of Newton Grange, mar. 1588, buried 1600.

Thomas, eldest son, obt. S. P. = Dorothy Alsop. — Roger, of Casterne, obt. about 1667, had three sons and three daughters. = Frances, dau. of Edmund Brudenell, of Stanton Wyville, co. Leicester, esq.

Nicholas Hurt, esq. of Casterne, buried 7th Feb. 1676, had three sons and four daughters. = Isabella, dau. of Sir Henry Harpur, of Calke, bart. — John of Uttoxeter. — Thomas, of Ilam, co. Stafford.

Nicholas Hurt, esq. of Casterne, bur. 1711, at Ilam. = Elizabeth, sister and heiress of John Lowe, esq. mar. 1670, bur. 1714.

Charles Hurt, esq. of Alderwasley, 2nd son and heir, bapt. 1678, a sheriff in 1712, bur. 1763. = Catherine, dau. of Gervase Rosell, esq. of Ratcliffe on Trent, Notts- bur. at Wirksworth, 2nd June, 1756. — Francis Hurt, gent. = Bridget, Rosell, sister of Catherine. — Grace, Mary, Mercy, and Catherine, all obt. S. P. — Thomas, John, Anthony, Henry, Elizabeth, and Dorothy.

Nicholas Hurt, esq. 2nd son and heir, bapt. 1710, bur. at Wirksworth, 11th May, 1767, S. P. — Francis Hurt, esq. of Alderwasley, brother and heir, died 7th Aug. 1783, æt. 61. = Mary, dau. of Thomas Gell, of Gatehouse, Wirksworth, died 6th March, 1801, æt. 81. — Grace, mar. 1749, Richard Milnes, esq. of Dunstan. — Charles, John, John, Gervis, Henry, — Mercy, Mercy, Mary, Catherine, Ann, Elizabeth, all died young or unmarried.

Francis Hurt, esq. Alderwasley, son and heir, bapt. 1753, died 5th Jan. 1801, æt. 41. = Elizabeth, dau. of James Shuttleworth, esq. of Gawthorpe, Lancashire, mar. 1778, living a widow at Derby, 1829. — Charles Hurt, esq. of Wirksworth, J. P. and D. Lieut. for co. Derby, sheriff in 1797, mar. Susanna, dau. of Sir Richard Arkwright, knt. — Catherine, mar. the Rev. George Holcombe, D. D. prebendary of Westminster, rector of Matlock, and of E. and W. Leake, Notts. — Cassandra, mar. her cousin, Philip Gell, esq. of Gatehouse, Wirksworth, but died S. P.

Mary, mar. Rev. Geo. Moore, of Appleby, in 1780, obt. S. P. — Elizabeth, mar. Thomas Webb Edge, esq. of Strelley, Notts. 1785, died leaving issue. — Mercy, obt. young.

Francis Hurt, esq. now of Alderwasley, of Aston on Trent, born 1781, sheriff in 1814, Just. of Peace, and Dep. Lieut. for co. Derby. = Elizabeth, eldest dau. of Richard Arkwright, esq. of Willersley. — James Hurt, esq. major in the army, born 1785, mar. 1825, his cousin Mary Margaret, 2nd dau. of Thomas Webb Edge, esq. Strelley, Notts. — Henry, a midshipman in the Hero, lost at sea, 24th Dec. 1811, S. P. — Mary, wife of Sir Richard Goodwin Kents, G. C. B. Vice Admiral of Red, &c. &c. — Elizabeth, mar. George Moores, esq. of Appleby and Snareston. — Cassandra, wife of Rev. J. F. Saint John, vicar of Spondon.

Catherine, mar. John Broadhurst, esq. Foston. — Cath. Emma, dead. — Ann Emma, living.

Francis Hurt, jun. esq. mar. at Bakewell, 22nd August, 1829. = Cecilia, dau. of Rich. and Lady Elizabeth Norman, and niece to the Duke of Rutland. — Mary, wife of the Hon. and Rev. Robt. Eden, of Hortingfordbury, Herts. — Emma, Elizabeth, Selina. — Frances, Anne. — Catherine, dead.

APPENDIX IV
List of prizes for Market Traders,

WHEREAS this Place having from the Establishment of large Manufactories therein become much more popular than heretofore, it is now necessary to form some Plan, whereby the People of the Neighbourhood may be induced to resort hither. and bring for Sale, on the SATURDAY in every Week, the Necessaries of Life, for the Use of the Inhabitants of CROMFORD and its Vicinity, the following PREMIUMS are offered as an encouragement to those Persons who may be desirous of becoming Candidates for the PRIZES below; and they are requested to give in their Names to Mr. BARK, at the GREYHOUND Inn, on or before the 12th Day of JUNE 1790, on which Day the Meeting will commence.

N.B. All Persons to give an Account of what they bring for Sale; and no one will be allowed to buy and sell any Commodity on the same Day, as that would be considered as selling with Intent to gain the Premium.

	£	s.	d.
THE Person who brings and sells, in a retail Way, the greatest Quantity of Beef and Veal on the SATURDAY in every Week, for One whole year, will be entitled to one eight Day's Clock, Mahogany Case, value	9	0	0
The Person who brings and sells the second greatest Quantity of Beef and Veal as above, will be entitled to one Four-post Bed with Green Hangings, value	6	16	0
The Person who brings and sells the greatest Quantity of Bread as above, will be entitled to one thirty Hours Clock, Oak Case, value	4	4	0
The Person who brings and sells the second greatest Quantity of Bread as above, will be entitled to Half a Dozen Joiners Chairs, and two Elbow ditto, value	3	1	0
The Person who brings and sells the greatest Quantity of Oatmeal, as above, will be entitled to one Mahogany Chest of Drawers, value	2	11	6
The Person who brings and sells the second greatest Quantity of Oatmeal as above, will be entitled to one half-headed Bed with Blue Hangings, value	2	5	0
The Person who brings and sells the greatest Quantity of Mutton and Pork as above, will be entitled to one Oak Chest of Drawers, value	2	2	0
The Person who brings and sells the greatest Quantity of Flour as above, will be entiled to one Mahogany Snap Table, value	1	5	0
The Person who brings and sells the greatest quantity of Bacon as above, will be entitled to Half a Dozen Turners' Chairs, value	0	19	0
The Person who brings and sells the greatest Quantity of Cheese as above, will be entitled to one square Oak Dining Table, value	0	18	0
The Person who brings and sells the greatest Quantity of Butter and Eggs as above, will be entitled to one large Looking-Glass, gilt Frame, value	0	18	0
The Person who brings and sells the greatest quantity of Garden Stuff as above, will be entitled to one Oak Snap Table, value	0	11	0

The Goods to be seen at the Greyhound Inn.

All Goods brought, and Sales made of them, to be entered in a Book (to be kept for that Purpose) at the Greyhound Inn, the beginning and close of each Day. Any Disputes arising between the Parties shall be finally determined by Mr. BARK, who is to be governed by the Book kept for the above-mentioned Purpose.

APPENDIX V
Incumbents of the Parish Church of St Mary, Cromford

1797	Reverend Richard Ward
1838	Reverend Robert M Jones
1886	Reverend William Henry Arkwright
1894	Reverend Egbert Hacking
1899	Canon George Henry Sing
1901	Reverend Alfred Thomas Humphreys
1915	Reverend George Arthur Hazlehurst Rural Dean of Wirksworth Honorary Canon of Derby Cathedral
1941	Reverend Cyril Brailsford
1949	Reverend Frank Samuel James
1954	Reverend Stephen Thomas Jones
1958	Reverend Christopher Holditch Read
1964	Reverend Laurence Henry Wood
1970	Reverend Harold John Lowndes
1988	Canon Harold Collard
1992	Canon John Wheatley Price

Richard Ward was a curate from Wirksworth who was "put in charge" of St Mary's Chapel, Cromford, as was Robert Morgan Jones, until a district was assigned to the church in 1869, when Richard Morgan Jones became the first vicar of Cromford.

After 1954, the living was held in plurality with St James, Bonsall, the Reverends Jones, Read, Wood and Lowndes being rectors of Bonsall.

Sadly the Reverend Lowndes died whilst in office on 10th November, 1988, after which the vicar of Holy Trinity, Matlock Bath was made the Priest in Charge of St Mary, Cromford and St James, Bonsall.

A United Benefice was approved on 24th November, 1994 which combined the two churches of St Mary, Cromford and the Holy trinity, Matlock Bath. The Reverend John W Price was made Priest in Charge and was the first vicar of the United Benefice.

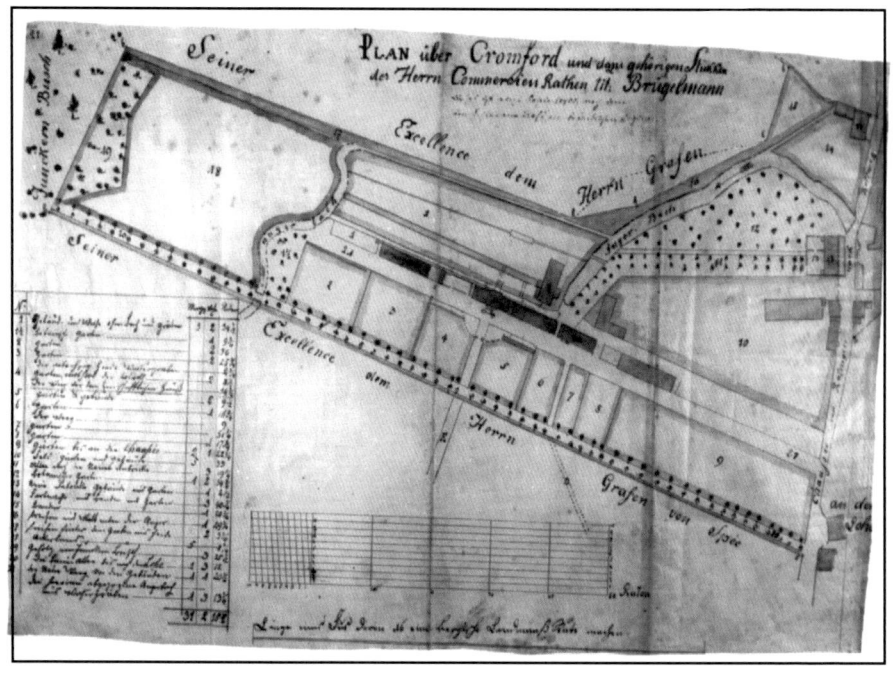

Cromford in Ratingen, Germany
Courtesy of the Hauptstaatsarchiv, Dusseldorf.

APPENDIX VI

Cromford in Germany

A Johann Gottfried Brugelmann, copied both Arkwright's machines and mill (on the site of an old grist mill) and equipped it at Ratingen, then a small and impoverished town near Dusseldorf, Germany. It has been recorded that Brugelmann's father copied the machines and methods, a more likely explanation is that Brugelmann enticed some of Arkwright's workers to emigrate to Germany, where they copied the machines from their own notes. An early instance of industrial espionage.

This mill operated at Cromford Mill from 1783/4 until 1977 when it closed. A factory school was built in 1835 and a later Brugelmann built himself a fine house, a "manor" just as Arkwright did. The effect of all this was that the factory system was given a start in Germany and this mill is the oldest on the continent.

The site has been cleared of more recent buildings, leaving the original mill and manager's house. The wheel has been duplicated as well as facsimiles of Arkwright's throstle and carding machines, which work from the water wheel. The copying of the machines was undertaken by a clockmaker, Charles Haycock of Ashbourne, Derbyshire using the originals in the Helmshore Museum of the Textile Industry, Lancashire as models.

The mill and house opened as an industrial museum on 2nd September, 1996
They have published a superb book (a Katalog), available in German only, the title when translated reads, "The first factory at Ratingen and Cromford".

The address of this enterprise is:
Rheiniszhes Indusrie Museum
Cromford Allee 24
40878
Ratingen
Germany

Telephone: 00 49 2102 87 03 09
The director is Dr Bolenz

This mill is part of a greater museum covering German industry and is well worth a visit.

The writer is indebted to Rheinisches Indusytriemuseum, Ratingen for their help and the Hauptstaatsarchiv, Dusseldorf for permission to reproduce the plan.

APPENDIX VII
Original water sources for Cromford

Today all the water used by the village is piped from the Severn-Trent Water supply, being part of the Derwent Valley Scheme.

Before this was undertaken, the water used by the village came from the following sources:

Black Rock Spring:

        670 feet O.D.   17,000 gallons/day
        204m O.D.   54 litres/m

Cromford Moor Spring:

        402 feet O.D.   91,500 gallons/day
        123m O.D.   291 litres/m

Rogelum or Roguelen Spring:

        520 feet O.D.   11,500 gallons/day
        158m O.D.   37 litres/m

Willow Well Spring:

        430 feet O.D.   40,000 galls/day
        131m O.D.   127 litres/m

All gauged in 1926 except the Cromford Moor Spring which was estimated.

A further spring in the parish fed the lower parts of Matlock Bath.

Birch Wood, Railway End. Output not measured but could keep a 4" (102mm) diameter main running full bore.

APPENDIX VIII

War Memorials
Cromford

Located in the memorial garden on the corner of Cromford Hill and Derby Road, Allen Hill side.

The inscription reads:
"In imperishable memory of the men of Cromford who gave the supreme sacrifice in the great War 1914-1919"

and

"Their name liveth for evermore"

1914-19	1939-45
Thomas Gratton	William A R Foster
John Hall Gregory	Harold F Britland
Harry Parker	David Graham
Samuel George Pearson	Denys G Marsden
Norman Saint	Kenneth A Brookes
Joseph Thomas Shaw	Michael G Hann
John Allen Taylor	Harry Rolley
Leonard Wilbraham	Alan G Ditchfield
Frank G A Arkwright	Ronald Hopkinson
Percy Barber	James A Tait
William Bosley	
Robt Charles Britland	
John Hall Brown	
Clifford James Brooke	
Vicor James Dillon	
Thomas Fearn	
James Gibbs	

Scarthin

Located on Scarthin Promenade overlooking the mill pond

The inscription reads:
"Erected to the memory of the men of Scarthin who gave their lives in the Great European War 1914-1918"

and

"May their reward be as great as their sacrifice"

1914-1918	1939-1945
Joseph Tomlinson	Harry Kniveton
William Sherratt	George A Pidcock
Arthur Biddulph	Arthur H Russell
Thomas Keightly	
Thomas Worthy	
William H Allen	
John J Allen	
George Kirk	
John A Pidcock	

Also worthy of record is the bench on the Derby road side of the memorial garden which is dedicated to:

"Seat in memory of 'Billy' Mee 1903-1997
The last blacksmith in Cromford
With thanks for 82 years service
From the people of the Village"

There is a memorial in the Community Centre to Margaret Wilson whose idea this was and saw it through until her untimely death.

Places to Visit

Most of the places mentioned in this book, maybe surprisingly, exist for us to see today, although some may no longer be used for their original purposes.

As the Honourable Byng said: Cromford is a "crowded village with cottages, supported by three magnificent cotton mills. There is so much water, so much rock, so much population and so much wood that it looks like a Chinese town."

Mills and machinery:

- Arkwright's Upper and Lower Mills along with warehouses, form part of the Arkwright Centre on Mill Lane. There are shops on the site as well as a cafeteria. The site is under development and is well interpreted.

- Masson Mill has been converted into a shopping village complete with a museum which houses an Arkwright throstle. The outside can be viewed from the main road, A6T, a few hundred yards north of Scarthin Nick. A plaque advises us:

    1769-1969
    200 YEARS OF
    SERVICE TO INDUSTRY

    and:

    SIR RICHARD ARKWRIGHT & CO
    ESTABLISHED, 1769

- Arkwright's original Nottingham Mill can be viewed from the bottom of Woolpack Lane, The Lace Market, Nottingham

- The school master's house where Arkwright's early experiments took place is now an Arkwright Heritage Centre, Preston, Lancashire

- An original Arkwright throstle which worked at Cromford can be seen in the Museum of the Lancashire Textile Industry, High Mill, Helmshore, Lancs. But alas not working. This throstle was acquired by Platt Bros and Co Ltd of Oldham and presented by TMM (Research) Limited.

- An Arkwright carding machine of 1775 and a water frame from the 1770s, both from Cromford, are at the British Museum of Science, London

Cromford Canal

- The feeder from the mill can be seen at the side of Mill Lane opposite the roadside warehouse.

- The original wharf and basin is available for inspection with an adjoining car park. A canal barge is to be seen here along with other canal memorabilia. A shop has been established here also.

- The canal proper can be viewed by walking from the wharf mentioned above for a mile south, where the visitor will find the High Peak Junction wharf where the Cromford and High Peak Railway connected with the Cromford Canal. The workshops are open to the public. The original engine shed still has its pit with cast iron fish belly rails (with C&HPR cast on and made by Samuel Wharton, iron founder of Tapton, Chesterfield), a blacksmith's forge complete with tools and with a cut-out on the entrance arch for the funnel of the locomotives. Some locomotives were built in this workshop. There is a superb audio visual display which shows a film of the railway when in use. On the canal side can be seen a wharfing shed.

- Also near to High Peak Junction can be seen the 1849 Leawood pumping engine house. This pump is put into steam on Steam Days, about four times a year.

- Just beyond the engine house one can walk over the Wigley Aqueduct. A steep climb down the river bank will allow the visitor to see the arches and cattle creeps.

- To the east beyond the aqueduct the Nightingale Arm can be seen, now weed choked.

- Continue along the canal to the Leawood Tunnel which can be negotiated with care by walking along the tow path.

Cromford and High Peak Railway

- This can be accessed either from the High Peak Junction or at the Black Rocks Picnic Site. The visitor is entreated to walk along the track from the Black Rocks or up Sheep Pasture Incline from the canal and view the village from above. The engine house, sans engine, can be viewed at the top of the Sheep Pasture Incline. To see one of the engines, the only one to survive, a visit to Middleton Top Visitor Centre is necessary. This engine was built by the Butterley Company in 1825 and worked until 1963. This is operated by compressed air on certain days.

- At the bottom of the Sheep Pasture Incline can be seen a catch pit complete with a half buried wagon.
- It should be noted that the old railway bed is now an amenity and can be travelled on foot, horse back or bicycle.

Buildings - houses are separate:
- Willersley castle is now a holiday centre for the Methodist Guild. They welcome visitors to use their tea room.
- Rock House is private and visitors are not welcome, however a view can be had from the High Peak Trail near to the Black Rocks and a limited view can be had from Mill Lane below the house.
- Cromford Bridge House or Hall is viewable from both Willersley Lane or Lea Lane. Access is not possible, it is currently partly used as a playgroup for infant children.
- Alison House is now a conference centre belonging to Toc-H. Contrary to popular belief, there is no right of way through the grounds.
- St Mary's Church is kept locked because of vandalism suffered in the past. The plate is kept elsewhere for this reason. Services are held most Sundays, see the notice board at the church gate.
- St Mark's Cemetery is all that remains of this church.
- Of the remaining chapels, the following are:
    Methodist Church and schoolrooms, Water Lane, still in use
    Chapel on Scarthin Promenade facing the pond is now an engineering works
    Chapel on Scarthin Promenade facing away from the pond is a private house
    Chapel at the bottom of Chapel Hill is a sorry sight. It is used as a motor repair workshop and has been much altered without any deference to its architecture or original use, but not by the present owners.
- The bridge chapel, on the west bank of the river and on the Cromford side of the bridge can be accessed best from Cromford Meadows. Note the squint in the riverside wall.
- Adjacent to the chapel is the Fishing Temple, note the Gothic inscription, Piscatorium Sacrum.
- The bridge itself can be viewed from downstream from the bank to Cromford Meadows or from the upstream from the bank close to the church. Note the pointed and semi-circular arches. The stone which

records the leap of the mare can be seen in the parapet near to the chapel, this is not its original location. By looking carefully in the water from the road over the second arch upstream can be seen the stone paviors on the river bed from which the depth of the river was measured by a measuring rod.

♦   The vicarage, close to Alison House is now occupied by a computer specialist and is also on private property.

♦   Arkwright's Corn Mill, destined to become an interpretative centre, is located at the end of Water Lane opposite the motor repair shop. Follow the path up the steps and across the front of a mill dam.

♦   The barytes and paint mill is on Water Lane and is used as a warehouse and sales place for basketware. The mill wheel still turns if only erratically. The owner should be commended for putting this back into workmanship after a long interval of idleness.

Lead Mining and Lime Burning

♦   Cromford Sough portal is in the Bear Pit to the rear of the shops at the bottom of Cromford Hill. A further portal is a feeder from the Mill Pond, the outlet can be seen along with sluice gates etc.

♦   Cromford Moor Mine site is at the Black Rock Picnic Site but all that remains apart from some depleted walls is the stump of a chimney, possibly the one used for the steam engine of 1922 and the concrete cap with a grille over the shaft.

♦   A careful look at the face of Dean Quarry, best viewed from the High Peak Trail near to Black Rocks will show the occasional lead working, in the form of a cave like aperture.

♦   The rock on Allen's Hill behind the war memorial has excavations formed by lead miners in its face.

♦   The mounds of spoil from the Bullestree Pasture Mine are evident on the hillside above the river on the eastern side.

♦   A lime kiln can be seen in a field at the top of Cromford Hill above Dean Quarry, this is on private land.

Water courses

♦   The major water courses are below ground but there is still much to see:

- The Mill Pond between Water Lane and Scarthin Promenade can be viewed from either of these thoroughfares. From Scarthin Promenade it is possible to view the outflow before it vanishes into a tunnel at the side and to the rear of the Greyhound Hotel. The supply is from the mill race from the paint mill wheel.

- The supply from the mill pond comes to the surface by the war memorial and does not reappear until it reaches the mill yard.

- The outflow of Cromford Sough both in the Bear Pit and as feeder to the canal has already been mentioned.

- The 1821 aqueduct across Mill Lane can be seen from the footpath and a discreet climb up the steps off the roadside opposite to the mill will reveal the top of the aqueduct and the part water filled leat.

- The original supply from the sough can be seen as a dry ditch from the main road, A6, as the leat passes under the base of the rock on Allen's Hill.- there is a series of dams with weirs at the side of Bonsall Hollow from the building known as Slinter Cottage, originally Arkwright's spindle mill.

Houses

- For an example of Arkwright houses at their best a visit to North street is a must.

- Further Arkwright houses can be seen on Cromford hill, some good examples can also been seen adjacent to the Greyhound Hotel.

- Via Gellia House, 16, Chapel Hill was the home of the Wheatcrofts who played such a large part in the life of the village from the time of Arkwright onwards. It was built by Nathaniel Wheatcroft in 1780. The original house also included number 18.

- Also on Chapel Hill is a house with a large balcony with a ground floor which has the appearance of a small warehouse. This was a Methodist Training College for the ministry.

- The row of cottages at the far end of Scarthin Promenade and known as Staffordshire Row were incorrectly reputed to have been built to house workers for the mills imported from the County of Stafford.

Other buildings and sites:

- Of the brick works and smelting works there is nothing to be seen

- Black Rocks, once known as the Stonnis, are well worth a visit and a climb to the top gives a rewarding panorama, but care should be taken, these rocks are dangerous. There is much graffiti, some of it from long ago.

- The white material running up the side of the rocks is the spoil tip from Cromford Moor Mine below. One can find an occasional piece of galena here.

- At the top of this spoil tip one can access Barrel Edge Quarry, now given over to nature. An abandoned imperfect millstone can be seen here.

- Inns and public houses:

    The Greyhound Hotel sits square overlooking Cromford Market Place
    The Bell Inn can be seen on the corner of North Street and Cromford Hill
    The Boat Inn is at the Market Place end of Scarthin Promenade

- Cromford Market Place is obvious to all, resident and visitor alike. To be noted are the single story stone and slate roofed market stalls and shambles, now filled in and in use.

- The village lock-up having two cells can be seen near to the Bear Pit

- The Bede Houses can be seen on Bedehouse Lane. Access inside is not possible as these are now private residences.

- Opposite Tor View Rise and on Cromford Hill are the cottages known as Hangman's Row, overlooked by a hill called Hang-on-High.

- War memorials - there are two, one for Cromford in a garden at the junction of Cromford Hill and the A6T, for the fallen of Cromford, and another for the fallen of Scarthin on Scarthin Promenade. The names of the Cromford dead can also be seen in St Mary's Church.

- The meeting hall on Cromford Hill opposite North Street was built by Peter Arkwright as a Working Mens' Institute, originally comprising a Reading Room and Meeting Place.

- The school at the far end of North street was built by Richard Arkwright junior. The two buildings for boys and girls can be seen along with the residence for the head teacher.

Abroad

Cromford (or Kromford) Mill at Ratingen near Dusseldorf, Germany was established on Arkwright principals by an ex-worker from Cromford, England in 1783. This has a throstle and other machines made by an Ashbourne man.

A walk around the Cromford Area

This area abounds in mines, mostly for lead but Baryte and Fluorspar were also found in quantity. Caution must be taken with these mines, open or poorly protected shafts abound and adits should not be explored without the help of experts.

A convenient point to start this walk is at the local authority car park on Mill Lane, Cromford, where a small fee is payable. It also has the advantage of toilets and a cafeteria in then old mill buildings opposite. The car park on the old Market Place in the village is usually crowded and is difficult of access and egress.

When talking of or walking about Cromford one cannot ignore the influence of the Arkwright family and the founder of that dynasty, Sir Richard. This subject is well covered elsewhere and is not discussed in this chapter except where the mines are concerned.

Leaving the car park, turn right to the church of St Mary, close to the 15th century bridge, widened in the 18th, having round arches on one side and pointed on the other. Hard by this bridge are the ruins of a bridge (or ford) chapel, complete with a squint where a light was placed before crossing the ford which predated the bridge. This ford, traces of which can still be seen in the water of the River Derwent which it traversed, dating from Roman times, for it falls on the route of Hereward Street. The ford lines up with the squint. Note the fishing "temple" close to the chapel.

Look over the second arch from the arch from the church end of the bridge, upstream, where will be seen the stone paviors where they dipped the water level.

The church stands on the site originally known as the Green, where a lead smelter stood. The surrounding ground is still poisoned for it supports very little vegetation even now. It is believed that a church stood here before the smelter, this is unlikely, these references are more likely to refer to the bridge chapel. The village which served the smelter, Willersley, stood close by and against the cliff which lies upstream of the river on the west bank. The smelter which used a water wheel in the river to drive its bellows, was cleared away by Arkwright along with the village, to make space for his church and to get the buildings and people out of view from his mansion, Willersley Castle. Two pigs of lead of Roman origin were found in this churchyard in 1912, which suggests that this could have been a smelting site for many centuries.

Close by can be seen the mills and warehouses built by Arkwright. One of the reasons he chose this spot, cheap labour and remoteness from the Luddites apart, was the availability of sufficient water to keep the mill wheels turning through both summer and winter, not to dry up during the former or freeze during the latter. He combined the Bonsall Brook, a plentiful source with the Cromford Sough which was a little thermal.

Retrace your steps from the church and walk up Mill Lane until you come to an iron aqueduct which crosses the lane and having the date 1821. This carried the sough water across the lane and into the mill, it is now dry.

Continue along the lane, passing the manager's house on the left and to the right of a private drive to Rock House. Rock House can be seen above a cliff overlooking the feeder to the canal. Continue to the cross roads having traffic lights. This is where the A6T road crosses the original route of Hereward Street and Cromford Hill can be seen ahead. The A6T road was originally the Derby to Manchester turnpike. Cross the road by the lights controlled crossing, this is a dangerous spot. The cutting through the limestone called Scarthin Nick can now be seen. The earlier cutting was undertaken to divert the carriageway away from Willersley.

Continue towards the Market Place, overlooked by the Greyhound Hotel, built in town hall style by Arkwright. The water from the Bonsall Brook is stored in a mill dam which lies behind this hotel which can be viewed from Scarthin promenade by proceeding behind the market shambles. The outlet flows underground into a culvert to the side of the hotel. Before the waters were diverted underground, they collected in a large pool where the market place now stands. The water appears briefly in the memorial garden opposite.

The cliff behind the memorial garden on Allen's Hill has evidence of lead mining trials, appearing as caves. At the foot of the cliff can still be seen the leat which connected the sough to the mill. Caution must be taken here as there are frequent rock falls from this cliff and they happen without warning.

Continue along the road away from the market place until you come to an opening between a café and a ladies outfitter, until you arrive at a circular enclosure, known locally as the Bear Pit. It is easy to see inside the pit, where you will see a desultory flow of water emitting from a tunnel, this is all that can be seen of the original Cromford Sough, mined between 1673-82. Its original portal discharged into the pond which stood where the Market Place now is.

Return to the main road which should be crossed to appropriately named Water Lane. Continue along this road, the motor cycle dealer occupies the original wheelwright's shop – note the Kiwi fruit vine growing on the wall - until you come to a building with a large iron water wheel. This is usually turning but does note drive machinery. This mill is where coloured earths were ground to produce pigments as well as baryte, it is now a basketware warehouse. Alabaster Sough discharges into this same race. The Alabaster Sough drained a mine of the same name, the vein being higher up the hillside. This vein produced a quantity of gypsum.

Continue along the lane passing a lorry depot on your left take short path on your left over a mill dam and you will pass behind the Arkwright corn mill, noting the wheel pit. This was where, before Arkwright, calamine - an oxide of zinc - was roasted and ground by the Cheadle Brass Company who built the mill on the site of the original manorial corn mill. The terrace of houses apposite called Staffordshire Row were built by this company for its workers.

Return to the Market Place by walking along the other bank of the millpond, called Scarthin Promenade. Scarthin is a separate community from Cromford as it falls in the parish of Matlock Bath. You will note the war memorial to the dead of this hamlet.

It is rewarding to stand in the Market Place and note the numerous Arkwright houses, built to his design and having three floors, the top one being for frame work knitters or stockingers, for his mills produced thread only. Most but not all of the smaller cottages predate Arkwright. It will quickly be realised that his effect on the village was profound. Looking up Cromford Hill, one can easily imagine the Romans travelling along it. Try and imagine the activity of the soughers and lead miners on this same hillside, which would have had many steams of water both clean and dirty from the soughs and from their buddles when washing the ore.

The numerous trees in the valleys hereabouts were planted by Richard Arkwright Jnr as a crop for spindle making. Of course they were never cut due to the failure of spinning. The Norman Frith being replanted thus turning the clock back, but what a superb asset these are now being mostly deciduous, albeit being badly managed.

Retrace you steps to the main road again and turn towards Matlock. Cross at the crossing and continue through Scarthin Nick until you come to an iron gate. This is the original one placed here by Arkwright and the rubble from the gate house can be seen. Continue a little further to enjoy one of the best vantage points for surveying Willersley Castle with the river below, a spot much loved by Eric Morecambe who enjoyed fly fishing here before his untimely death.

Cromford Court can be seen across the road, hidden partly by trees. Continue further on and you will arrive at Mason Mill, noticeable in red brick rather than the local stone.

Return to your car along the river side of Scarthin nick which will bring you to the church and the car park.

Distance about 1.5 miles and allow an hour or so.

The Leap of Mr. B.H. Mare, June 1697. (Author)

The Fishing Temple

Wheatcroft's Depot -(Author)

Cromford Bridge Hall

Mary Barton of Cromford, 1829-1918, as Mary Stokely, New York USA, 1860 (Author's Collection) See page 90

Bibliography

Abbreviations:

BCA	Book Club Associates
DAS	Derbyshire Archaeology Society
DRS	Derbyshire Record Society
HMSO	His Majesty's Stationary Office (1929)
PDMHS	Peak District Mines Historical Society

Adam, Wm	Gem of the Peak, 5th Ed. 1851 Reprinted Hartington, 1973	
Bayles F and Ede, Janet	The Cromford Guide	Cromford, 1994

Bulletin of the Peak District Mines Historical Society:

Volume 2, Number 2, October, 1993
The Peak District in the Great Exhibition
    Ford T D

Volume 4, Number 2, December, 1969
Lead Mining in the Wirksworth District during
the late Eighteenth and early Nineteenth Centuries
    F S Ottery

Volume 4, Number 3, May, 1970
Report of a field meeting held on Sunday, 21st
September, 1969 at Cromford Meadows, Derbyshire
    Gregory, Neville

Volume 5, Number 5, April, 1974
Lead Mining in the Cromford Liberty (1698-1714)
    Flindall R

Volume 6, Number 6, December, 1977
Wind, Water and Steam Power on Derbyshire Lead Mines,
    A List.   Willies L, Rieuwerts J H, Flindall R F.

Volume 8, Number 3, Summer, 1982
The early lead mining industry and the ancient
desmenesne of the Peak   Daniel, Martin

Volume 8, Number 5, Summer, 1983
Volume 8, Number 6, Winter, 1983
Cromford Sough and the early use of Gunpowder
    Rieuwerts J H

Volume 10, Number 1, Summer, 1987
John Burton of Bonsall, Derbyshire and Iowa, USA,
1795-1854   Naylor P.J.

Briggs, Asa	A Social History of England	BCA, 1983
Cooper, Brian and Neville	Transformation of a Valley	Cromford, 1991
Craven M & Stanley M	The Derbyshire Country House	Derby, 1982
ditto	Volume 2	Derby, 1984

Dodd, AE and EM	Peakland Roads and Trackways	Hartington, 1974
Farey, John	General View of the Agriculture of Derbyshire Vols. 1-111 London, 1811-17	
Fitton, R.S.	The Arkwrights - Spinners of Fortune	Manchester, 1989
Frith J B	Highways and Byways in Derbyshire	London, 1920
Heath, John	Illustrated History of Derbyshire	Buckingham, 1982
Kiernan, David	The Derbyshire Lead Industry in the Sixteenth Century	DRS, 1989
Lake, Hazel	The Arkwrights and Harlow	Harlow, 1996
Mee, Arthur	The King's England, Derbyshire	London, 1974
Monet-Lane Harry C	The Romans in Derbyshire Vol.2	Bolsover, 1986
Morris John Ed:	The Domesday Book, Derbyshire	Chichester, 1978
Naylor, P J	Ancient Wells and Springs of Derbyshire	Cromford, 1983
Naylor, P J	Celtic Derbyshire	Derby, 1984
Nixon, Frank	Industrial Archaeology of Derbyshire	Newton Abbot, 1969
Pevsner, Nikolaus	The Buildings of England, Derbyshire	Harmondsworth, 1978
Rieuwerts J.H.	History and Gazetteer of the Lead Mine Soughs of Derbyshire	Sheffield, 1987
Stephens J.V.	Wells and Springs of Derbyshire	HMSO, 1929
Stokes Arthur H	Lead and Lead Mining in Derbyshire	PDMHS 1964
Swanton M. Ed:	The Anglo-Saxon Chronicle	London, 1996
Tomkins, Rodney	Pipe Organs of the Derbyshire Derwent	Cromford, 1995
Uttley, Alison	Our Village	Cromford, 1987
Womens' Institute, Federation of	The Derbyshire Village Book	Derby and Newbury, 1991

Maps:

Burdett's Map of Derbyshire, 1791
DAS, 1975
Map of Roman Britain - Third Edition　　　　Ordnance Survey, 1956
Matlock (South) - Pathfinder Series SK 25/35　　Ordnance Survey, 1979

Records;

1841 Census for Cromford and parts of Matlock Bath　　Derbyshire Library Service

Acknowledgements

The following people, friends and strangers alike, have been of considerable help in writing this book, some of whom were unstinting in the trouble taken in trying to please a trying and pedantic researcher:

The Parochial Church Council for St Mary's, Cromford
Mrs Radford of the County Library Service, Matlock - ever helpful, ever courteous
Brian Smith of Cromford
Bill Pepper, warden of Alison House
Mr D R Wilson, University of Cambridge, Committee for Aerial Photography
David Bick of Newent, Glocs.
Jean Housley of Cromford
Roy Paulson of Lea
Margaret Elson of Matlock